MW00768768

To Jeri Blackburn, with appreciation for your friendship and in admiration for your strong and positive christian witness!!

New Millennium Families

How **You** Can Soar Above the Coming Flood of Change

MICHAEL C. BLACKWELL

May 8,

Parkway Publishers, Inc.
Boone, North Carolina

Michael C. Blackwell

Parkway Publishers, Inc.
P.O. Box 3678
Boone, North Carolina 28607

Library of Congress Cataloging-in-Publication Data

Blackwell, Michael C.
New millennium families : how to soar above the coming flood of
change / Michael C. Blackwell.
    p. cm.
    ISBN 1-887905-21-9
    1. Family life—United States. 2. Social change—United States. 3.
Family—Religious life—United States. 4. Family—United States—
Forecasting. I. Title.

HQ535 .B53 1999
306.85'0973—dc21   99-048420

layout and design by Julie Shissler
editing by Patty Wheeler
cover design by Bill May, Jr.

To my wife
Mary Catherine Kanipe Blackwell
and our two wonderful children
Julie R. Blackwell and Michael C. Blackwell, Jr.

And in loving memory of my parents
Clitus S. Blackwell and Viola Maness Blackwell
and my in-laws
Jack E. Kanipe and Mildred Deal Kanipe

TABLE OF CONTENTS

Prologue and Acknowledgments

"And the waters prevailed exceedingly upon the earth; and all the high hills that were under the whole heaven were covered...And the waters prevailed upon the earth 150 days." –The Book of Genesis

As the fall of 1999 turned into the winter and spring of 2000, thousands of people in eastern North Carolina were still reeling from the worst floods to ever hit the state.

The physical damage reached billions of dollars. Crops, homes, animals, churches, human lives— and one entire community — were wiped out as rivers and creeks overflowed their banks following back-to-back hurricanes Dennis and Floyd.

Psychologically and emotionally, many residents still suffer from the floods. A heavy rainstorm frightens many people to the point of panic. Young children especially have grown scared of water; such was the sense of fright and fear inflicted by the floods.

The metaphor of the flood is what this book is about. Floods surround us. They threaten to undo us. Nowhere is the coming flood of change more ominous than in the basic unit of society: the family.

The purpose of *New Millennium Families* is to offer a roadmap of encouragement and hope to families facing their own personal floods, and to say, "You can soar above whatever flood that comes your way." Soaring demands work, commitment, trust, and discipline, but it can turn a flood of disaster into a rainbow of hope.

Let the adventure begin!

Since 1965, I have had the privilege of working with children, youth, and families. They have been my greatest teachers, and I owe them much for their inspirations and life-lessons.

My immediate and extended family always offer support to whatever "impossible dream" I undertake.

Rao Aluri, president of Parkway Publishers, has been a friend and guide throughout this process. Patty Nash Wheeler, my college classmate, strengthened the book with her editorial guidance.

Craig Bird of the Baptist Children's Homes communications staff patiently assisted with constant revisions and gave wings to my words when I needed them most.

Jennie Counts, my executive assistant, was the glue that held the whole project together, especially when it threatened to come unglued. Her positive critique of the manuscript and her constant upbeat spirit with everyone who assisted me is greatly appreciated.

Paul and Hunt Broyhill of the Broyhill Family Foundation in Lenoir, N.C., have been valued advisors for two decades. The Foundation's support of *New Millennium Families* has made wider distribution possible, and I am grateful.

To my mentors, friends, employees, parishioners, trustees, and most especially, the children and alumni of The Baptist Children's Homes of North Carolina, I say a heartfelt THANKS! Royalties from *New Millennium Families* will be donated to worthy causes.

Finally, I express profound gratitude to William Friday, president of the University of North Carolina for 30 years and a dear and cherished friend, for writing the Foreword to *New Millennium Families*.

Michael C. Blackwell
Thomasville, N.C.

Foreword

True prophets, unlike fortune tellers, do more than predict the future. Much more.

In fact "what is going to happen" primarily functions as a hook to get people's attention. A true prophet, like those of the Old Testament, analyzes the situation, sees where society is headed unless change occurs at a basic level, and proposes correctives.

Michael Blackwell is a true prophet, and my friend of 40 years.

From his longtime vantage point as head of the largest child care organization in the state, The Baptist Children's Homes of North Carolina, and from a heart dedicated to helping hurting children and healing broken families, Michael has pondered the state of the American family. The sociological statistics he quotes gain flesh and blood and bone through the wounded eyes of children and family members he and his staff look into daily. The suggestions he makes reflect reality, not abstract theory. It brings me great comfort that he feels the dire straits of the American family need not be permanent.

Like the Old Testament prophets, he weeps over the destruction and ruin of what God intended the family to be. Like them, he calls for a return to basic actions—what once upon a time would have been called common sense—fully aware of modern social and economic realities. Like them, he is ultimately optimistic for the future of the family.

As you read and apply the concepts of *New Millennium Families* to yourself and your own family, you will have moments of inspiration and illumination: "I can do that and things will improve!" Michael calls us—as husbands and wives, parents and children, friends and mentors—to do what is right and do it consistently. He calls us to soar above the flood of change marking the 21st century and shows us how to get wind beneath our wings.

Specific suggestions on "how" to invest time with your children, "how" to get along with your spouse and your mother-in-law, "how" the church needs to support divorced parents, even "how" to pick out a quality day care and "how" to simplify your life—it's all here.

As a fellow North Carolinian—he from Gastonia, I from Dallas (Yes, there is a Dallas, North Carolina)—I have seen firsthand as a trustee the good things Michael and The Baptist Children's Homes of North Carolina do for children and families. It is a Christ-like, God-honoring work.

New Millennium Families: How You can Soar above the Coming Flood of Change makes the potential for such good widely available. It is my prayer that countless lives and families will be influenced by it and that God will be honored and our children nurtured to their potential because of it.

William Friday
President Emeritus
The University of North Carolina
Chapel Hill, NC

Introduction

The Family Glory Train:
   ### facing the New Millennium
   ### with soaring confidence

Every day I see flesh-and-blood examples of children and families whose lives have been salvaged and redeemed.

Geana is one such child. And she just keeps growing. Not long ago Geana addressed a group of children's advocates on behalf of Baptist Children's Homes of North Carolina (BCH). She stood tall and spoke like a pro. In the crowded conference room, Geana found a receptive audience who hung on her every word.

Born to a prostitute in Reno, Nevada, the courts revoked her mother's parental rights when she was eight months old. Though divorced from Geana's mother, her father took custody and raised her alone for six years until he remarried.

 Although her relationship with her father was strong, Geana constantly battled her stepmother. "We had problems right away," she explained. "She blamed a lot of our problems on my dad, saying he didn't punish me or discipline me right. Our personalities conflicted."

Her family also had a secret everyone knew--except Geana herself. When she spoke of being excluded from family pictures without being told why, I almost wept. Finally, at age 12, she learned her biological mother had listed a former husband's name on her birth certificate, merely "to give me a name and a paper father."

Though she remained emotionally close to her "paper father," the blow understandably deepened her anger and conflicts escalated. "My stepmother and I were at each other all the time. She said she couldn't stand me anymore and didn't think she could continue to live with me," Geana said.

Though her parents did not regularly attend church, her Uncle Joe took her almost every week. She accepted Christ after a Sunday School class one morning. Despite that, "To verify what I thought was everyone's opinion of me, I got into trouble all the time. I started skipping school, sneaking out all night with my friends and stealing money from my aunt." Less than two years after unraveling the paternity secret, a "major blow-up" convinced everyone involved that the situation demanded outside assistance.

As arguments with her stepmother grew increasingly violent, suicide seemingly offered a good way out. But before she killed herself—or disappeared beneath the turbulent waters of the juvenile justice system— she attended a carnival.

Businessman Jim Goldston, an aggressive supporter of BCH, hosts an annual carnival at his business near Raleigh-Durham to raise funds for the child care and family ministry efforts. A distraught Geana showed up for the excitement and the rides—and learned about Baptist Children's Homes.

"Goldston's Carnival literally saved my life," she concluded. "We started discussing if Baptist Children's Homes might help and, after several weeks, we called. That's why I'm here. I hope someday I can tell whoever is responsible for it how much I appreciate what they do."

Unknown to her, she just had. Goldston, a BCH trustee, sat listening to her—tears in his eyes—just a few feet away. Later he told me he had been wondering if the benefits to children justified the time and effort of the carnival. "I got my answer loud and clear just now," he added.

The confused and angry adolescent who came to us turned her life around. Geana graduated from Thomasville (N.C.) High School, her impressive academic record earning her a full college scholarship. Ironically, the young girl who embezzled money from her aunt served as treasurer of two student associations at the school. Today, she walks and speaks with confidence, articulate and determined. She broke up her audience claiming she wants to be either an actress or a lawyer because "there's a lot of drama in both."

Convinced she now has "a bright future," she declared, "With God's help I can succeed in the career of my choice. BCH provided me with a chance to make amends with my family and to lead a normal and productive life."

Geana's story still thrills my soul. Her shining example shouts that young people are basically good, and that they can soar above the ashes of defeat and despair.

Children's homes and family service agencies exist to solve problems. Problems bring children into our care. They sometimes exhibit the very problems that brought them to us, until they gain control of those behaviors. They're trying hard. We're trying hard to help them.

Sometimes, when they get discouraged or the world seems to be crashing around them, they need affirmation. And, like our own children, they need it at the very time you are most aggravated with them.

When I give a hug, or hear a loving parent or surrogate say a positive word instead of the reprimand the child earned, I can see the relief and gratitude wash across their faces. Then, if you look with love and faith, you can see reflected in those faces the potential for more Geanas.

Nurturing that potential requires the cooperative efforts of a lot of people trying to live under and in God's grace. In fact, we have our own twist on the Biblical mandate to "train up children in the way they should go."

You see, about 30 trains of all descriptions roll by our Thomasville campus on a regular basis. Their whistles rattle cottage windows just a stone's throw away. One alumnus wrote that he felt like he could hang his feet out the window and have the train clip his toenails as it rolled by.

I tell you this like some proud engineer because it strikes me how train-like Baptist Children's Homes of North Carolina is—a place of hope and miracles whose mission is "helping hurting children...healing broken families."

One of the awesome characteristics of a train is its incredible momentum, even when traveling slowly. The combined forces of mass and forward motion mean it takes a train a long time to stop—and a lot to stop its progress.

Baptist Children's Homes has been building momentum since 1885. The positive combined mass of children and families, supporters, trustees, administration and staff, buildings, land, animals, and other assets has moved through the history of this state like a freight train, slow, steady, and mighty.

It has followed straight tracks of mission, still glistening with promise toward the horizon. Those tracks run true and Baptist Children's Homes' wheels are firmly seated on those tracks. We are about providing services to new millennium families, whatever form or shape they take, to help them deal with the issues that separate them and bring healing to their relationships.

Michael C. Blackwell

Holding those rails together are the firm ties of the trustees, solid and true. Our mission rests on their guidance and support. The rails don't separate or start to split off into odd directions because the trustees hold them together, on track.

Any engine needs fuel. Baptist Children's Homes' contributing individuals, churches, corporations, foundations, alumni, and families supply the fuel to keep this train rolling. Without them, we coast to a stop and this trip is over.

Passengers on this train are the children we serve and the families from which they spring. They board in all kinds of situations. Some are put on board by caretakers, some by family members; others jump on the train of their own accord. At first, they all sit by the window of their coaches, noses pressed against the glass, wondering how they got there and where they're going. What waits for them when the whistle blows and the conductor hands them their luggage and puts them off to begin another leg of their journey?

Child care and social workers are the conductors on this train. They walk the aisles and help passengers find their way. They direct lost passengers, provide blankets for comfort, and answer bewildering questions. The conductors nurture the passengers until they arrive.

And I'm the engineer, driving the locomotive, head out the window, one hand on the throttle, an eye on the track ahead. I've already lost my striped railroad cap to the wind, and we're moving on. I'm secure that our track, ties, and conductors work together for the well-being of all passengers.

Gifts, fears, needs, and hopes. They're all part of new millennium families. Whether you're running from failure or sprinting toward the finish line, climb aboard the Glory Train. The journey is just as much fun as the destination, the challenge as great as the winner's reward.

Chapter 1

Defining the promise: millennium family tree nearing bright dawn

> Govern a family
> as you would cook
> a small fish—very gently.
> — *Chinese proverb*

*I do not know what I may
  appear to the world
But to myself I seem but a boy
  playing on the seashore
Diverting myself now and then
Finding a prettier shell or
  a smoother pebble than before
While the great ocean of truth
Lays all undiscovered before me.*
—*Isaac Newton*

*The sun WILL
come up
tomorrow !*
—*Little Orphan Annie*

"As the twig is bent, so grows the tree." Perhaps your grandmother or favorite teacher quoted that proverb to you. It's true, you know. On tree farms, loblolly pines—safe from gangs of small boys genetically programmed to climb—mature straight and tall. The neighborhood tree, which as a sapling serves as a horse and seasonally donates limbs for homemade kite frames, never knows symmetry. Even on the calmest day, a coastal hardwood points the way the sea winds bend it. On mountaintops, gnarled evergreens tangle over themselves in search of soil and shelter.

The proverb is true—but it's not the whole truth. Because no matter how you bend the young willow, it will never be a redwood. An apple tree won't sprout oranges. Grown trees, like adult humans, reflect where they came from as well as where they've been. Hidden roots bind a tree to its heritage. The visible trunk and limbs yield to the sculpting of events.

Better: "As the twigs are bent, so grow the Family Trees. As the roots, so the seedlings—at birth—will be."

Admittedly, as our American "Family Forest" seizes the new millennium, there are far too many Family Trees in trouble. Otherwise, the Baptist Children's Homes of North Carolina (BCH) would not be straining to help thousands of hurting children and to heal their broken families. The blight of disappearing fathers, the fungus of drug abuse, and the drought of materialism twist and stunt. Family Trees splinter under hurricane winds of economic and social pressure and die inside out with dry rot from deceit and manipulation. Floods of change drown buds and wash free roots.

But neither would BCH invest its every resource in families and children unless we knew pain could be soothed, that families could be redeemed. Family Tree roots still probe deeply into rich soil of Christian heritage. There are vast vistas of healthy Family Trees when we lift up our gaze. The battle is engaged but certainly not lost. We can embrace the third millennium with an optimism informed by faith and sustained by hope.

My positive outlook rests on four assumptions:
1. People want to change for the better.
2. Other people can help people change.
3. As an individual, "I" can help others change.
4. God is the source of real, lasting change.

We can be better parents and children and husbands and wives, more constructive friends and neighbors, and employees and bosses. Some of the suggestions in the following chapters may be difficult—but none are complicated. We can save the Family Forest—one Family Tree at a time.

But just exactly what are we saving? What constitutes "family?" I'm glad you asked. "Family" is God-ordained, but self-defining.

While it is virtually impossible to arrive at a universally accepted definition of family, in the Judeo-Christian context family includes a loving adult or adults who strive mightily to raise children in a safe, wholesome environment in which they can thrive and come to know the God who created them and who loves them.

Of course you can have a family unit with two adults, who are neither parents nor intend to become parents. This contributes to the difficulty of defining family. Twenty-first century social scientists will struggle with definitions of family that don't necessarily include more than one adult, or whose members are of a single generation or gender. In America, "family" enjoys certain legal and tax benefits. Is the day upon us when anyone can claim himself/herself or a friendship group as a "family" and thus qualify for insurance and tax considerations, or claim discrimination if they are denied?

A friend of mine defines a family as "a group whose members are irrationally crazy about each other." Call me irrational, but by that definition—which I embrace—I'm "positively" crazy. To negative folks, the new millennium looms as a big dark cloud, portending evil. To the rest of us, it lights a big dark night and promises intrigue, challenge, and opportunity unlimited.

It won't be an easy time to raise a family, but then, I'm not sure there ever was an easy time. Earlier generations—especially those before 1910—suffered the agonies of burying many infants carried off by epidemics. My parents didn't think it easy rearing me in the textile village of Gastonia, N.C. My wife and I struggled rearing children in parsonages and in the glass houses of pastorates and public professions. Each generation faces challenges and learns to overcome them.

Did the "good old days" ever exist as the universal norm? We cannot fathom the difference in human existence in the broad but brief span between the end of the first millennium and the end of the second—just 1,000 years. Ten short centuries.

Think on these things—in the just-expired millennium: the now extinct Incas were developing a culture that conquered an incredible empire they ruled from Peru . . . Leif Erickson landed on the shores of North America with a band of Vikings . . . a newly-invented rigid collar gave horses four times the traction and improved the lives of subsistence farmers in Europe . . .in the Americas, the native peoples domesticated corn and made the first chocolate drinks.

During the first few centuries of the second millennium the Black Plague killed one European in four . . . the survivors beat back Arab invaders from the south and fought Mongol hordes from the east. From the beginning of the second millennium to its last hours, wars ravaged the populated continents. Family life was also difficult a thousand years ago.

Even one century past in America, children openly sewed clothes in sweatshops. A hundred years ago, coal-burning stoves choked the air and horse traffic clogged the streets, women couldn't vote, and water fountains were segregated in the South.

There were no telephones, airplanes, automobiles, computers, or satellites. We didn't have strawberries all year or CNN all day. There were no Social Security or disability payments for those too old or injured to work. And two catastrophic world wars, separated by the worldwide Great Depression, were still to come.

Do you suppose the grandparents of that era also told their children, "I'm glad I'm not starting a family at a time like this!"

Ah, but consider this: In 1900 Acquired Immune Deficiency Syndrome (AIDS) was unknown; few smoked; no automobiles turned into coffins for 50,000 casualties of highway accidents every year; our inner cities throbbed with vitality and hope. There were no gasoline shortages or electrical power outages; no "Y2K" fears; no suicidal bombers blowing up markets in Europe and schools in America.

So, while "family" sustains assaults at every turn today, I steadfastly cling to a realistic hope for families. History reveals "family" can survive tough times. Facts support my conviction, faith sustains it. Granted, the 1900 definition of family may not be the definition families of the 21st century use most frequently. In fact, the definition of the distant future may be closer to that of the distant past—more functional than biological, caregivers linked to both children and the elderly.

Perhaps the definition of "family" needs to be enlarged beyond the immediate circle of parents and children, to include relatives and even friends involved in the lives of the children we serve. An uncle in Baltimore may be more "family" than is a local dad who refuses to be involved with his child. A teacher may invest more time in a child than the biological mother may. In those situations, they help heal the family and sustain the young boy or girl.

But by any definition, "family" is society's building block. Our media depict very few whole, healthy families in the sense that tradition defines them and I think best: loving married male and female parents in a home, caring for each other, and mutually nurturing their children in a family relationship that requires commitment — and perhaps sacrifice.

When movies or television do portray such "ideal" families, they often display them as objects of ridicule or disdain. Plainly, healthy families have disappeared as an entertainment concept, but only from minds and marketing strategies of media executives who think the only things that sell are sex and violence. Heartwarming stories of family life, particularly those showing families overcoming challenges, are scarce (though Christian film critic Phil Boatwright reports that the average profit of "G" movies is higher than the average for the deluge of "R" releases).

The tight, gravitational pull of family members toward each other keeps our society from simply flying off the face of the earth under the centrifugal forces of a culture spinning out of control.

With all the negatives, is there still hope for families?

Yes! I'm wildly enthusiastic about new millennium families. I want them to soar above the coming flood of change. Here are a few reasons why they will:

The Family is God's creation.

Who would give up hope in something God created and declared good? That's why we see every child at Baptist Children's Homes not as a problem child, but as a child with problems. We don't abandon hope. Each child and each family, lovingly formed by a loving Creator, fits into God's plan. God created man and woman and joined them together, for fellowship and for family. Even when families fail and children are damaged, God's grace can bring good out of evil.

God remains in control.

Some people say society is in bad shape because evil dominates. The Bible acknowledges evil but tells us that, ultimately, God is in control. The sun rising this morning told me the same thing, as did children waiting at the bus stop, the dogwoods blooming in season, and my dog licking my hand.

There is order in the world. Bad things, terrible things, happen but God's natural order moves time and space in a consistent pattern. Love begets love; smiles multiply; consistency in child rearing is rewarded; hugs melt defiance; tomorrow comes. Having crested the new millennium, the measuring rod of all history remains the same. God is still in control.

Good family models still exist.

Look around. Someone you know holds to a standard that promises positive results. Kids on the honor roll volunteer at the hospital, study in the library, sacrifice summers in volunteer missions, work hard at home, school, and church. Most parents are diligent in their duties, delaying selfish goals and leading young people as volunteers in school, church, and neighborhoods. Someone, lots of "someones," model and encourage such behavior. This tells me the standard is not lost.

I urge you to consciously support young families in their efforts. If your family is solid, mentor a young couple just starting out. Help that family anticipate the rough spots and be there to steady their boat.

The very flux and turmoil of the American family in this transitional epoch provide opportunity for the next great step forward as adults react to the mess around them by making the creation of a healthy family a priority.

Life and its elements undergo swings to the extremes. Since the American family seems near the peak of the negative extreme, the pendulum has begun to swing the other way. Who would have thought the longhaired tie-dyed shirt and bell-bottom jeans-wearing protesters of the 1960s would become conservative business people driving a booming new millennium economy? Who would have thought their children would be more conservative than their parents?

The Church hasn't given up.

Churches daily strive to provide positive answers to the question, "What can you do for my children?" without succumbing to the notion that church is just for children.

Many parents seek a "positive socialization and values education" for their children. Often they don't realize that the best answer lies in their response to the question, "What can the church do to help parents enjoy a close, personal, meaningful relationship with God?"

Churches are absolutely pro-family. Clergy know the most positive way to support the family is to provide each member with a nurturing circle of spiritual friends who can encourage, challenge, and support their common journey toward God.

The Church is more accepting of "flawed" families than in the past, making it more willing and more able to minister to hurting families. Not long ago, divorced persons felt cast out from the Church. Today churches are taking the lead in divorce recovery, single parent classes, day care, job-networking groups, physical fitness to go with spiritual fitness, marriage retreats, couple times, and classes to help adults gain parenting skills. Those that don't, should.

Because the Church has "the answer" to all questions of significance in the person of Jesus Christ, it is sometimes slow to respond to new questions. But family issues light up the night sky like the "rocket's red glare." When "dawn's early light" breaks, the Church will be found standing by the shore, ready—as always—to carry on.

Vital, strong family health organizations

Focus on the Family is one of the best known of dozens of organizations that work to help and preserve families. Others include Council on Contemporary Families, National Council on Family Relations, Council of Family and Child Caring Agencies, American Family Policy Institute, Christian Family Ministries, Family Research Council, UpAmerica, The Alliance for Children and Families, and more.

Child care agencies like Baptist Children's Homes of North Carolina have expanded services and emphasis to families. We position ourselves as "child centered, family focused." Children come into our care after abuse, neglect, abandonment, rebellion, death, broken marriages, and related issues force the family to separate for the good of its members. While child care workers in the cottages help the children work through their issues and deal with their part of the problem, social workers deal with other members of the family to help them resolve the issues from their perspective.

When the children in our care meet their goals, they return to a family which also has had to meet specific goals and is measurably healthier than when the children left it.

Leigh Ann's first stay at our Kinston, N.C. campus lasted just a few minutes. On admission day she walked in the front door of the administration building and, as soon as her parents drove away, she walked right out the back door and kept on going. Police found her that night and brought her back.

Escalating and debilitating family struggles forced her into our care. She smoked marijuana "every day in the eighth grade" and the once good reader tested virtually illiterate from drug use. She railed against authority and cursed her mother and stepfather.

Her self-image rested almost solely in being "tough." There was no place for tears or compassion. "I would never cry," she recalls. "I was angry at the world and I didn't care about anybody but myself. I wouldn't let anyone hurt me."

But Leigh Ann learned both to let people help her and to help other people. Her friendship with April provided a framework where they challenged each other on bad behavior and destructive attitudes. "Helping people helped me make progress," Leigh Ann points out. April, who orchestrated school fights, did drugs, continuously ran away from school and home, and was blatantly promiscuous in an attempt to devastate her parents by getting pregnant, agrees: "We learned to control ourselves."

Staff members and other girls in their group confronted the girls, too, and helped them see that their parents' rules were motivated by love, not for a desire to control or belittle them.

The program that helped April and Leigh Ann allows a boy or girl to "apply for graduation" when they feel they have a solid grasp on their problems and their solution.

The process requires them to admit and write down the problems that brought them there, state the improvements they have already made, write about the help each group member has given them, and document the help they have given to others in the group.

It's a long, self-searching process but it helps each boy or girl realistically gauge his or her progress.

Applications for graduation (transition from the behavior modification program) must be approved by the peer group before they can be passed on to the staff for action.

"It helped to realize that everyone has problems, no matter how perfect they act and that there are constructive, positive ways to work on them so they don't destroy you," Leigh Ann explains. Learning to cry "without feeling prissy or silly" marked a milestone for Leigh Ann. "It is important to be able to cry because it's a way to get out your feelings," she says. "Sometimes you can cry even when you're happy."

On a home visit as Leigh Ann explained to her mother some of the things she had learned about her problems, "my mom started crying— I thought I hurt her. But they were tears of joy."

Her parents too were working through a structured process and progressing toward a shared goal with Leigh Ann—a stable family environment.

I am renewed every time I see young people express themselves like Leigh Ann and April. They come to us sullen and angry, holding hurts inside until those hurts threaten to eat their way out.

Then they learn to release the hurts gently, with tears and talk, and lay the groundwork for a new life, a fresh start. It's a beautiful thing and it's what keeps me beating the drum for BCH and the family values it practices and preaches.

Can you see yourself in this picture? As fewer people throw up their hands over the way things are, and more people roll up their sleeves to change the way things are, I become ever more encouraged about the future of families.

A family is an organism, a living, breathing entity with a life to preserve, a future to secure, a destiny to claim. God is in control and my hopes, dreams, and convictions are positive. New Millennium Families, under God's leadership, can bridge the troubled waters threatening them. Together we can soar above the coming flood of change.

Chapter Two

Who's doing what to whom: things old, things new in family relationships

My parents don't always make
the best decisions,
but to me, they are
the best at what they do.
—Nancy, BCH child

The family that has taffy-pulls together, sticks together.
—Grandma Soderquist

The bumper sticker left no room for discussion. "If my music is too loud," it declared in bright, bold letters, "you're too old." It awakened faint echoes of a mantra of my generation: "Never trust anyone over 30" and the final words of Paul Newman in the movie *Cool Hand Luke*: "What we have here is a failure to communicate."

The teenage boy of the blaring bass and window-rattling beat entered and left my hearing in a matter of seconds. But what about his family? Were any of them excluded from judging any of his actions? Did generational factions occupy mutually hostile warring camps labeled "under 30" and "over 30"? Were most conversations failed communication, "full of sound and fury, signifying nothing"?

If so, pity that family.

The family traditionally has been the strongest cultural force and greatest influence on teens, but family is changing. Divorce impacts 3,000 children per day, and 40 percent of U.S. children will at some time live in a home without a father present. Homefront problems also are compounded by workaholic parents, sexual abuse, alcoholism and drugs, and the "latchkey" syndrome of children who are at home while both parents work.

The response to the cry of the changing family is to build relationships that are accepting and loving, and then model for them healthy families. Which begs the question, "What constitutes healthy families?"

Michael C. Blackwell

What is a 'family?'

Christian author Gary Smalley's description resonates with me. Smalley says a healthy family consistently depicts six elements:

- Members exhibit a high degree of appreciation for each other.
- They spend considerable time together.
- There is open communication among members.
- They share a strong sense of mutual commitment.
- Their common life is marked by a high degree of spiritual orientation, and
- They are able to deal with crisis in a positive, constructive manner.

Note the interrelatedness of the second and third attributes—"time together" and "communication." If your family is going to be something more than boarders in a common building, you must make time and communication priorities. If parents deprive each other and their children of face time so they can work night and day to provide "things," they may find no one there when they have "arrived."

Smalley's perspective, like BCH's, is unabashedly Christian. But even secular family therapists generally recognize the following elements in any unit defined as a "family:" rules, roles, boundaries, distribution, and communication (in some form) among members.

Thus a group of people living together does not function as a family if rules and boundaries are not understood and enforced, if roles are not clearly defined (even if flexible), power is not shared (though not equally), and there are no clearly understood methods to negotiate differences between parents and children. Christianity adds that healthy families should have a spiritual center, appreciate and spend a lot of time with each other, pursue common goals, and deal with conflict in productive ways.

All this presupposes a parental authority figure or figures—even if it's an older sibling, stepparent, foster parent, etc.

Is parenting limited to conception?

Until the late 1990's the vital role parent figures played in child development and family stability was pretty much accepted as a given. Then New Jersey grandmother and psychology textbook writer Judith Rich Harris tilted at that windmill in *The Nurture Assumption*. Claiming that nothing you do or do not do will make a bit of difference to the kind of adult your child becomes—not in temperament, character, personality, or intelligence—Harris argued the idea is wrong "that what influences children's development is how their parents bring them up."

Harris based her study on analysis of scientific research, especially studies of twins. She says, for instance, that identical twins reared in the same home are no more alike than those reared apart. And two children adopted by the same parents turn out no more alike than a duo raised separately.

Excuse me? Did she say the only contribution parents make to the adult their child becomes is their genes? Implications of her perceptions could be profound, among them an "absolution" of sorts for bad parents who cheat their children of time and themselves.

I'm much more inclined to side with Dr. T. Berry Brazelton, professor of pediatrics at Harvard Medical School, who argues that "the basis for all learning, social and cognitive, is laid down by parents in the first years of a child's life." At least that's been the common wisdom since parents first cautioned children not to drink whiskey so they won't end up like Uncle Otis. Or for parents who sit for hours reading to their children so they will love books; or throw baseballs until their arms drop off so they have a better chance at making the team.

Certainly peer influence is stronger than in earlier times but on any given day, I can give you the names of hundreds of boys and girls currently served by BCH and thousands of our alumni whose very scars and nightmares testify to the impact their parents had on them. Names like Lacey and Jason and Janete.

Many will carry to their graves the emotional wounds and put-downs that still pierce their souls.

At 13, Lacey lived in a van on a beach with her father and four brothers and sisters. Weeks earlier her mother had permanently abandoned her 14-year marriage and her children to move in with her boyfriend. Her parents' violent arguments and disappearances had marked Lacey's entire life. Like her parental models, Lacey verbally and physically battled her older sister and three younger siblings as well as her mother; she became truant and even attempted suicide.

Before Jason was a teenager, he bounced through seven foster homes prior to settling in with his grandmother. Eight years earlier she had promised his dying father to raise him and keep him away from his drug-addicted mother. But one day Jason's mom stormed the house, dragging Jason's grandmother by the hair as she held a broken bottle to her neck, threatening to kill her if Jason didn't come with her.

Janete's life, always difficult in her poor neighborhood in Brazil, turned horrible one traumatic afternoon. Her drunken father staggered home with a can of gasoline and matches and burned himself to death, Janete's mother fled, taking three of her children with her but abandoning nine-year-old Janete and her brother. An American couple adopted the siblings but for four years Janete turned her hurt and anger at them, even threatening their newborn baby.

Lacey, Jason, and Janete all wound up at Baptist Children's Homes. Counseling, Christian role models, structure, and help in setting and working toward goals became part of their lives. They learned to "deal" with the traumas inflicted by their parents, to be successful and productive. But their darkest dreams always recall images of violence, and every relationship they enter struggles under the handicap of still-fragile, rebuilt trust.

For decades behavioral genetics—the field that examines how much heredity shapes personality—has said that genes account for maybe half of the differences in people. Where does the other half come from? Try parents and the weight of all they do and say and teach.

Nature tells us that much. Almost anyone who contemplates the question realizes the powerful influence of parents to effect good or evil in the personalities of their children, and the influence of other environmental factors such as selection of friends, religion, education, encouragement, and opportunity.

Let me offer another example: intensive studies of differences in student learning argue convincingly that educational success is not determined simply by the quality of one's gene pool or by which side of the tracks one lives on. While factors such as per-pupil spending, school size, and teacher experience and training have measurable effects, they all pale in comparison to the influence of family environment and background.

I will continue to support the idea that family environment greatly influences the development of a child. A child's destiny is not determined at the moment sperm and egg collide.

I'll have what they're having

Peer influences flow from and feed on media such as music, television, movies, computer games, and popular literature. So it can be argued that the media influence today's children more than parents, siblings, schools, friends, or church—and sometimes more than all of them combined. We're told that the "average" teen listens to four hours of music per day (doesn't that seem low by about 10 hours?!) and will see 23,000 hours of TV by high school graduation. By making it their business to understand the issues and emotions of youth and to shape their economic desires, the media control the "maps of reality" by which children and teenagers navigate their world.

Of course it would be foolish arrogance to think "only kids" twist and turn in the winds of music and movies, art and advertising. All segments of American society are saturated by media messages, many of which tempt us to be unsatisfied with who we are and entice us to blur moral distinctions.

Adults and youth live in a world where increasingly more people believe absolute truth cannot be known. Our age declares that each individual determines what's right and wrong in the context of a particular moment. Some estimates are that 60 percent of Americans don't believe in absolute truth. In that context families may no longer accept moral authority simply because "the Bible says." But the research—and the children who sleep in the cottages at Baptist Children's Homes—would argue that human beings need boundaries and that some things are wrong simply because they are wrong! Youth need a response to their cry that clearly and firmly explains truth in language and cultural images that they can understand. But before adults can speak that answer with validity and integrity, they must make those truths operable in their own lives.

Many youth today have no hope for the future, as evidenced by projections that up to 20 percent of them will attempt suicide. Such hopelessness, which also stalks all age segments of the population, provides the church with a door of opportunity to offer hope through a relationship with God.

New Millennium teens show promise

Life in the hallways may be changing.

Teenagers live in the hallways of their schools, in the mallways of their shopping centers. For adults with no teenagers at home, the gaggles of ill-dressed teens congealing around the movie house doors and food court tables may be the only image they ever see of the breed.

This is an age that adults see as consumed with a chase for a unique identity, and every teenager finds his or her uniqueness in the same trendy shops and hair salons. As one comedian told them, "Remember, you're unique. Just like everyone else."

But some observers are proclaiming that the shallow pursuit of "belonging" and popularity and "fitting in" is running out of steam. Leaking away, too, is the trademark of too-cool-to-care youth.

Whether in community service or the arts, in schoolwork or personal relationships, millions of teens are demonstrating a seriousness and a compassion that have drawn the attention of marketers, opinion research groups, mass-media producers, and experts on generational issues.

Gerald Celente, director of the Trends Research Institute in Rhinebeck, N.Y., says today's teens "will pick up where the '60s revolution left off." The members of Generation Y are loosely defined as those born after 1980. In 2005, the group will be the largest teen population in U.S. history, numbering 39.7 million.

As with every generation, this new one has its share of cynics and slackers. But national surveys indicate a shift away from the "too cool to care" posturings attributed to members of Generation X. The Y's have grown up immersed in the cynicism of Chevy Chase and Madonna, *Seinfeld* and *Saturday Night Live*, negative political campaigns, and music centered on "what-difference-does-it-make" themes.

Teenagers in care at Baptist Children's Homes demonstrate that new earnestness. A cottage group at Broyhill Home in Clyde, N.C., visits the father of one of their peers, who is confined to a nursing home.

In Thomasville, Mills Home young people make sandwiches for Habitat for Humanity construction workers and help clean up one of the building sites. Others visit local senior adult day care centers and turn the jail parking lot into a free car wash for police cars. Cameron Boys Camp (Cameron) residents have raked and cleaned yards. Kennedy Home (Kinston) and Odum Home (Pembroke) residents are actively involved in nursing home visitation and lending a hand to others.

Residents of our homes across the state stretch themselves to be involved in other lives. They all are learning the benefits of service.

Stretching outside themselves helps the teenagers, who come from troubled situations themselves, recognize how fortunate they are to be in a situation where they are safe, have plenty to eat and nice clothes to wear, and where authentic adults love them and are helping them through a difficult period in their lives.

They're not alone.

A 1999 national survey asked nearly 3,000 teens "What makes a good leader?" A majority listed "honesty," "not being afraid to speak up," "being mature," and "having a strong moral character" as important. The root of society's problems, they said, is "selfishness — people not thinking of the rights of others."

The survey uncovered a new twist among teens: personal accountability. A majority blamed their own peers for problems in schools. They said it's up to students, along with teachers and parents, to be part of the solution.

Yet, the harsh slap of reality also was evident in the survey. The teens said the most pressing problems include child abuse, AIDS, the abduction of children, pollution, and homelessness.

What's moving teenagers toward this sense of earnestness? Oddly enough, it could be maybe the most maligned generation of teenagers ever — those who came of age in the '60s. These baby-boomer/parents are close to their Generation Y children and have passed down values of idealism and activism. Generation Y and the boomers seem to agree on important issues, whether they have to do with authority, environment, the corporation, government, or volunteerism," says Celente, adding, "I can't find any tie in history when there's been so much agreement between two generations."

Kids are getting more freedom from parents and feel more at ease in the world. However, without an anchor securing them to home, this freedom in the world can be more frightening than exhilarating.

As a child, I remember when a trip to Charlotte from Gastonia was a big deal. I loved the tall buildings, but wanted my dad's hand where I could clutch it, too.

Today kids hop into their own cars and zoom across the state to see a concert. While teaching my kids to drive, I was amazed they knew area streets better than I did.

On the one hand kids seem to recognize risky behaviors. On the other, their seemingly "moth-to-flame" attraction to drugs, alcohol, and cigarettes distresses me. They have studied issues of sexuality and substance abuse as early as grade school, but knowledge of dangerous behaviors doesn't keep as many teens from taking those risks as I would wish.

Today's teens have a sense of empowerment as well. It comes not just from their large numbers and big economic impact, but also because they are adept at new technology and sophisticated in understanding the spin of advertising and the media.

Generation Y teens feel they can control their destinies. Thus empowered, they are more proactive. They can see the value of parental input to get good grades, walk the straight line, stand up for values.

That's encouraging.

Their parents might still find their music too loud, age differences will continue to provide fertile soil for generational distrust, and there will be failures to communicate. But New Millennium Families have plenty to smile about.

Chapter Three

Lord, is it I?
As a matter
of fact, it is!

It is not the mountain
we conquer
but ourselves.
        —Sir Edmund Hillary

> *We can't let the pain continue to gain.*
> *We can't leave here the same.*
> *It's time to make a change.*
> *We can't let the day be the same*
> *As the times now behind,*
> *The day we leave shouldn't*
> *be the same as the day we came.*
>   *- Maria, BCH child*

When my children were youngsters, I often reminded them to bring their bicycles inside where the weather wouldn't fade and rust them, and where careless pedestrians and backing cars couldn't bend them. "Important things often are fragile," I emphasized. "We have to take care of the good things with which we are blessed."

Another frequent discussion occurred after dark. Too often I couldn't get the children into bed because they wanted to watch television longer or play more games or just be up with their mother and me. I preached the importance of "a good night's sleep"—then I studied into the wee hours or returned home from meetings long after the tube had cooled from *The Tonight Show.*

I told my children and my congregations not to be careless with their bodies because they receive only one from the Gracious Provider. Then too often, I would let my body take temporary control over who I am, and it made the authentic "me" suffer.

Health is a gift of God that enables us to enjoy God's most precious gift—time. Without health, every hour seems a week; every year a lifetime. When healthy, precious hours pass productively and meaningfully in the fluttering of an eye. Isn't it strange to consider our hectic schedules driving us through day after day, tugging at us like a riptide dragging a struggling swimmer out to sea? We pack our calendars so tightly we know there isn't room for another single event or thought.

Then we pick up a flu bug and can't lift our heads off the pillow. All the terribly important things we were going to do suddenly become insignificant in light of our desire to simply lie there and get well.

And on our sick bed a new thought claims a spot on our agenda: how come I always get sick and other folks don't? Does it seem to you that some people are just born healthy? It's true to a limited extent. But beginning from whatever level of health your genetic heritage gifted you, you can nurture, protect, and improve your personal health with some caring attention.

Here are a few "do's" and "don'ts" to help you keep your body healthy:

Proactive Positives

Just start doing it. When you begin a new exercise regime, start slowly. Get a physical checkup before you begin a program if you haven't been exercising. Then pick activities you enjoy. Find a partner. Knowing someone is waiting and depending on you will pull you out of bed many mornings when it's still dark and cold. I used to jog with a church deacon every morning at seven o'clock. (And those years when he was deacon chairman, I usually let him beat me!)

Walking is the easiest "starter" exercise. All you need is a good pair of shoes. You can do it anytime, day or night, without having to drive anywhere. Thirty minutes a day, three times a week will get you started and show quick results in how you feel.

Exercise is a proven way to build your body's immune system. People who regularly exercise get sick less often than those who don't. Why? Because exercise produces chemicals in your body to keep you healthy. Just by becoming more physically active, you increase your production of healthy chemical messengers—tiny proteins—circulating in your body taking the good news to every cell in your body. But you have to get off the couch and onto the trail, court, or gym to make it happen. Yet, in spite of modern knowledge that exercise is essential to a long and healthy life, people declare they don't have time to exercise. How can this be? It's like my children leaving their bicycles out in the weather. They didn't "have time" to put them on the porch, so the bicycles became rusted, or ruined.

How can you "not have time" to care for God's gift—your precious health—a gift that enables you to enjoy your years on earth?

Eat at home

Restaurant food often is high in fats and sugar. If this weren't bad enough, many restaurants now serve huge buffets. Given the prevalence of obesity, this trend will require added diligence and discipline by their patrons.

However, it's difficult to blame anyone besides ourselves for any unwelcome weight gain. Until we assume full responsibility for what goes down our throats, we can't realistically hope to live a healthy life. The most effective way is to eat at home where we can better control the ingredients going into our food. It is encouraging, however, that many restaurants have become health conscious, and offer delicious, well-balanced meals. That's good news for those of us who travel a lot, or who simply enjoy the relaxation of a good meal out.

I have struggled with weight issues most of my life, so—as I dispense this wisdom, I do so in front of a full-length mirror—just to keep me humble . . . and honest!

Eat fresh fruits and vegetables

With a global economy, fresh produce is available virtually year round. If eating an orange or apple with your breakfast seems expensive, cut back on your afternoon candy bar. The cents you save there can enrich your grocery fund so you can eat with sense every morning.

Support friends' efforts to eat healthy

Don't tease them for choosing an apple over chips or try to force second helpings or desserts on them. Often when we sabotage someone else's effort to "eat sensibly," we do so out of guilt, even if unconsciously. We don't like visual or verbal reminders of someone else's self-discipline when they remind us that we should walk away from the empty calories. But instead of doing what we should, we try to convince our friends to join us in our folly. Misery does indeed love company—even when it tastes wonderful!

Drink lots of water

Your first hunger pangs are often a sign not that you are hungry, but that you are thirsty. Dry lips are a symptom of low overall body hydration, so drink a glass of water; don't just apply lip balm.

The standard recommendation for adults is eight glasses a day. A single glass before each meal and at mid-morning, mid-afternoon, and bedtime takes care of six of those.

Keep healthy snacks around the house

The most convenient snack foods come in foil wrappers, but they are full of sugar and fat. When you slice an apple to go with your morning oatmeal, save a quarter of it in a plastic sandwich bag for a morning snack. Healthy foods are not usually the most convenient. But the little bit of preparation time, or clean up after peeling an orange, is well worth the health benefits.

Eat five small meals a day—but not of doughnuts, Danish pastries, and other fat-laden non-foods. A good breakfast, an apple or banana mid-morning, a sensible low-fat lunch, another fruit or vegetable snack mid-afternoon, followed by a nutritious early dinner rounds out a healthy day. This keeps your energy level high all day long. At the same time, it allows you to get rid of unwanted fat without ever feeling hungry.

Positive Prohibitions

Don't overeat

Among the best exercises you can do are "push-aways." Push yourself away from the table before you're stuffed. There is no sin in leaving food on your plate.

Never eat to fullness—just until you're no longer hungry. There is a difference! In most parts of the world, the American habit of eating meat three times a day is a reason for wonder. We consume many times the protein of the typical non-American, yet get winded climbing two flights of stairs. In Asia, South America, and Africa—when and where there is sufficient food—you'll find lots of children who wouldn't break a sweat mastering the President's Physical Fitness standards that fell so many American elementary students.

Don't let habit's demand for satisfaction determine how much you eat. Use three smart tactics to reduce your urge to eat more than you need: (a) drink more water before a meal, (b) consume all the healthy things first—fresh fruits and vegetables, and (c) eat slowly to give your body time to signal that it has had enough. Then, at the first feeling of satisfaction, push away.

Never eat in front of the television

When you eat, don't watch! Eating in front of the TV is a "filling ritual" because it makes you less aware of how much you're eating. And it encourages eating the notoriously fat-loaded and nutrition-empty snack foods. Worse yet, eating in front of the television massacres one of the most precious family bonding rituals, the time spent together at the dining table.

If TV terror stalks your home, causing your children to fight the idea of having dinner together, consider relieving the pressure with the VCR. Find ways to make having dinner with their parents an experience that's equally precious to your children. This means parenting by leading, by using the time to recognize and show respect for your children's interests and viewpoints. If dinner is always a recital of their shortcomings, or if you regard them as a captive audience for your monologues, your captives will find a way to escape.

Don't use alcoholic beverages

Yes, there was wine in the Bible. But powerful alcohol in its modern incarnation has wrecked so many homes and ruined so many lives, who can stand to defend it? To those of you who declare the health benefit of wine with "proof" from studies, I will simply say that later developments in those studies showed the real benefit came from the grapes used in the wine, not the fermented product itself.

Though I don't necessarily agree with her translation of the original Greek, I do think the elderly woman had the spirit of the issue when she debated the topic with her pastor. When the young man pointed out that Paul had advised Timothy "to take a little wine" for a stomach problem, she looked the preacher straight in the eye and declared, "He meant rub it on, not drink it!" Her knowledge of Greek is far surpassed by her knowledge that the Bible teaches us to take care of our bodies, and abstinence is a good way to do that as far as alcohol is concerned.

Don't use drugs

Of course, I'm talking primarily about non-prescription drugs. But you should also keep even prescription drugs to a minimum. As my doctor reminds me, "All prescription drugs are toxic to some extent." They are chemicals and chemicals mix and interact in unpredictable ways in your body. Drinking alcoholic beverages while taking prescription drugs is especially dangerous.

Illegal drugs, obviously, are known to have serious consequences— which is why they are illegal. While a few people manage to shake off addiction before it kills them, many are never able to escape from its brutalizing grasp. And there are many documented cases of someone being killed by his or her first experiment with an illegal drug.

Don't smoke

No one in America can still be ignorant of the consequences of using tobacco. In the 1960s a public service television ad asked the country, "Do you remember the first time you tried a cigarette?" As coughing battered the soundtrack, the announcer intoned, "Maybe your body was trying to tell you something." For decades everyone who purchased a package of smokes also purchased a printed warning of the danger. Folklore has it that the original Marlboro Man died from lung cancer.

The tobacco companies even introduced evidence of the common knowledge that smoking was destructive in their unsuccessful defense of liability lawsuits. At least one jury got to hear a recording of Phil Harris' hit from the 1940s, "Smoke, Smoke That Cigarette" about how you can "smoke, smoke, smoke 'til you smoke yourself to death" and you'll need "to tell Saint Peter at the Golden Gate that he's gonna hafta wait because I just gotta have another cigarette."

Tobacco attorneys also rightly pointed out that people had referred to cigarettes as "coffin nails" for decades, thereby acknowledging they willingly indulged in a dangerous habit.

Although not every smoker dies tragically because of tobacco use (smokers get run over by trucks, too), many horrible deaths are caused by smoking. My father died a smoker's painful death from emphysema, which is slow suffocation caused when the tiny air sacs in the lungs lose their ability to transfer oxygen to the blood.

Smoking is a distasteful habit that pollutes the environment of everyone in the vicinity. There is no way for a smoker, whose senses of smell and taste have been dramatically diminished by this habit, to understand this. But a person who does not smoke, and is never around smoke, is highly sensitive to the acrid residue clinging to a smoker.

What is that smoke doing to your lungs? Ask yourself about this the next time you see someone hobble along with an oxygen tank connected to his or her nose by a plastic tube, as at risk as a fish out of water. Tobacco does this to your lungs.

What does smoke do to your arteries? Think about this the next time you read about someone dying young from a heart attack. What is smoke doing to your body? To your skin, eyes, and nose? The several hundred poisonous chemicals in tobacco smoke are attacking your health in hundreds of different ways.

Men especially should be aware and concerned that smoking triples the chance of sexual impotence.

Barring accident, smoking not only will shorten your life by many years; it shortens the remaining years of your healthy, vigorous life. Whatever pleasure you might get from smoking a cigarette disappears with the last puff, but the damage to your prospects of living a long and healthy life stays in your body. If you smoke, stop. If you don't, laugh off any peer pressure you might feel to start—and gravitate toward friends who respect God's gift of health too much to waste it on a nicotine high and tar-swathed lungs.

A sick or dead spouse can't work on improving his or her marriage. A sick or dead parent can't provide children the care and attention they need. Your health is a special gift. Don't scorn it.

Chapter Four

To Be A Child:
like being a parent
it's fun, done right

Every child is born a genius.
                    —Buckminster Fuller

> *The soul is healed*
> *by being with children.*
>   *—Fyodor Dostoyevski*

> *I love you little.*
> *I love you lots.*
> *My love for you would fill 2 pots,*
> *15 buckets, 16 cans, 3 teapots,*
> *2 dishpans, and a lot more.*
>   *—Juan, BCH child*

Wordsworth claimed "the child is father to the man." Jesus said we have to "become like children" to get into the Kingdom of Heaven but Paul wrote of the need to "put away childish things." If men suffer from Peter Pan Syndrome, perhaps women are afflicted with Tinker Bell Syndrome. Often neither sex wants to grow up. Perennial rock star Rod Stewart is the unlikely troubadour for the AARP crowd when he sings "Forever Young."

The truth is, while being careful to distinguish between "childlike" and "childish," all humans are children at times throughout their lives. The age of the mourner weeping beside a parent's grave doesn't matter—it is the child that cries. A spectacular sunrise or the Technicolor displays North Carolina foliage puts on in the spring and fall are best appreciated by eyes of innocent wonder. Doesn't most of the best of life qualify for Hall of Fame catcher Roy Campanella's description of his career? "You have to be a man to play baseball—but you have to have a lot of little boy in you, too."

So as we rear our children and spoil our grandchildren, we need to be tuned to the child-parts of us and try hard to remember what situations look like through younger eyes and shorter perspectives.

About those dream walkers

One of the things I like most about my work is that I have been able to see dreams come true. We admire adults who dream and who are original thinkers. We wonder how they can see cities where prairie grass waves, how they can see a house on a truckload of bricks, or how they get beyond the "why?" of problems to the "why not?" of solutions. If such an adult seems a bit eccentric, we say she marches to a different drummer, call her a nonconformist, and marvel at her creativity.

In a child, these traits cause problems for most folks. We appreciate the childlike qualities in a genius but too often expect our children to act like mature adults. Do you worry if your child is forgetful, disorganized, and easily sidetracked? If a child is creative in ways unfamiliar to us, we're somehow uncomfortable. If she memorizes books or spends hours at the computer writing stories but can't sit still for homework, we wonder if there's a learning disability.

Maybe instead, you have a dreamer, someone professionals call a "divergent" learner. You may not know what to do with her. Perhaps we're talking about a child who's full of imagery but can't be bothered with the details of spelling correctly, or a child who is always focused on something but maybe not what you or the teacher or the rest of the class is focused on, or a child who's happy and well liked but easily distracted. When you ask her to do something, it's not that she doesn't hear you, or can't absorb it or forgets, experts say. Something else simply captured her attention and became more important.

Such children are frustrating, and even seem defiant and inconsiderate. They are creative and interesting but also can be disruptive and uncooperative. If adults do not engage them in learning, they can go "downhill" as early as first grade. The stories in their minds are more interesting than the classroom work. They seem disinterested or unattached mentally. While there may be a developmental disability, look at all aspects of the child's life before you "discount" him with a disability.

Parents also are likely to jump to the wrong conclusion when their expectations and a child's behaviors don't match. Helping this child begins with identifying her strengths and feeding into them. Developmental educators emphasize that parents must connect and build on the successes the child can see since the more visual reminders she has, the more she's likely to be able to take responsibility for herself.

When you feel on some days that all you do is shriek at her, you can be sure she feels that way, too. That hurts not only your relationship but also hurts her self-esteem as she gets the sense that it's wrong to be herself, that the way she thinks isn't a good way.

Professionals have a phrase for children who are non-conforming thinkers: "the Edison trait," an imagination that brings them into conflict with their world. Tell your child about Thomas Alva Edison. One of the most brilliant and productive citizens this country ever produced was thrown out of school but went on to great achievement. Such examples can make a dreamer feel good about herself.

Let's strive to give dreamers the freedom to dream big. Let's encourage dreams and pin feathers to the wings of dreams every day.

Suggestions for parents of dreamers

● Engage a dreamer in schoolwork by asking her to teach you something, or to tutor another student.

● Understand that because dreamers have such vivid imaginations, it's not unusual for them to go through periods of nighttime fears.

● Keep directions to a dreamer brief, specific, clear, and logical. That will keep "what-if" scenarios to a minimum.

● If it's hard to communicate with your dreamer, try using a pet as an intermediary: "I wonder what Spot thinks about this?" If your child answers for Spot, she's probably speaking about herself.

● Although dreamers need to have consequences and limits like any other child, an angry punitive response from a parent tends to push them further into their imagination. Be proactive whenever you can: "What can we do to help you remember not to forget?" When she does forget, present consequences firmly but kindly: "Keeping your sister waiting was inconsiderate. What can you do now?" When she tells you, "I don't know what happened," she means it. She was probably distracted and not paying attention.

Children's best chance for success

Of course parents do have responsibilities in addition to dream enhancement. Many practical activities provide structure for children and help them prepare physically and emotionally to reach their potential.

For example children fare best when parents establish regular bedtimes and a daily family routine.

- Monitor television viewing and other out-of-school activities.
- Express high but realistic expectations for achievement.
- Stimulate reading, writing, and discussions among family members.
- Help with homework and access to newspapers, encyclopedias, and other home-learning tools.
- Encourage use of libraries, museums, and other community resources.

Just as family interactions around the dinner table pay surprising dividends, the number and variety of learning tools (books, tapes, puzzles, encyclopedia sets, computers, and the like) in the home have a profound effect on student achievement. The number of learning tools available in the home is a much stronger predictor of academic achievement than factors such as whether parents expect children to attend college.

When someone raises a question no one around the dining table or sitting in the living room can answer, seize that opportunity to look it up on the Internet or in the encyclopedia. When a meteor shower is due in your neighborhood sky, watch it with your children. When you have guests, encourage them to tell about what they do and why it is important. Have game nights where you and your children hone wits and develop cognitive skills. Make it fun to grow mentally and it can become a lifetime habit.

Your home environment is definitely an influence on your child's development. Make it a positive one.

Where our children fail

The most important trend of our era is the declining well-being of children which is evident in a number of areas, including health and the changing family structure.

The report card on youth health qualifies our country for grounding and/or detention—America's young people are barely passing. The

American Health Foundation gives children and adolescents a "C-" on their overall health. The annual Youth Health Report Card is not good news.

Children and adolescents continue to hurt themselves by using tobacco, alcohol, and illegal drugs; leading sedentary lifestyles; and eating too much dietary fat. For many of us who can remember "recess" as a much-anticipated activity, the report says that only 42 percent now participate in daily school physical education programs.

Too many young people are contracting avoidable infections, have high cholesterol, or have become victims of sexually transmitted diseases.

Foundation president Ernst Wynder puts it bluntly: "America certainly cannot point to the cumulative below-average grade with any sense of pride or accomplishment." He hopes that the "report card" is a wake-up call for parents, health educators, and others who are responsible for conveying a message of preventive medicine to children/youth.

One fourth of U.S. children are overweight, which earned them a "C" in that area. Five-year-old and six-year-old children earned three "A's" and one "B" for a high rate of immunizations from measles, mumps, rubella, DPT, and polio. The Foundation gave out four "F's"; one was for the number of black females under 18 years old who became pregnant and another was for the low numbers of black teenagers who received prenatal care during pregnancy.

Other failing grades were given for the high numbers of youths aged 10 to 19 who are murdered or injured by firearms. More than 4,000 children each year are homicide victims, the Foundation said.

The Foundation's grades for the youth of America include:

"C" for cigarette smoking. Seventeen percent of high school seniors reported daily smoking during a 30-day period.

"C" for marijuana use. Twenty-two percent of high school seniors reported smoking marijuana.

"C" for drinking. Twenty-eight percent of high school seniors had five or more drinks on one occasion during a two-week period.

"D" for child abuse. There were almost three million reports of child abuse and neglect in most years of the 1990s, almost double the numbers reported in the 1980s. Statistics are not expected to improve anytime soon.

These alarming statistics go hand in hand with many other reports on America's youth. The bipartisan National Commission on Children wrote in one of its reports that addressing the unmet needs of American youth "is a national imperative as compelling as an armed attack or a natural disaster." We may have the first generation of children and youth in our history who are less well off—psychologically, socially, morally, and economically—than their parents were at the same age. This does not bode well for new millennium families.

Exactly what is it about the changing American family that is a problem? Many believe it is that the marriage bond is steadily weakening. Children are spending less time with their parents for many reasons. The child-centered, two-parent family has growing signs of disintegration reflected in the high divorce rate and growth in the number of unwed parents. Such changes are a central cause of rising individual and social problems in our society: delinquency and crime, including the alarming juvenile homicide rate, drug and alcohol use, suicide, depression, eating disorders, and the growing numbers of children in poverty.

Still, while we focus on the problems in order to understand the solutions, we can take great courage in the fact that there are solutions within our grasp. Even more encouraging are the majority—a vast majority—of our children who are good, and kind, and positive.

Those blessedly short teen years

It is tempting—but dangerous—to judge how much your children "need" you by either what they can and can't do or by what they say.

It's obvious that a helpless infant, without the strength to roll over or hold a bottle to its mouth, would quickly wither without your attention. And most parents devote much of themselves to their infant children.

But as the child grows into adolescence, parents feel more freedom to return attention to their own careers, confident that "Johnny and Susie" are making their way toward teenage and adulthood just fine. While they wouldn't miss a parent/teacher meeting or a school program in the first few grades, middle school teachers often see lots of empty seats.

So, these parents miss warning signs that their adolescent needs them and is in danger of irrevocably damaging his or her life—a closed door, wrong friends, bad grades, defiant attitudes.

For years I have striven to alert anyone within shouting distance to the danger in slighting our adolescent generation. I truly believe America is neglecting its 19 million young adolescents to such an extent that half of them may be permanently hindering their chances for productive and healthy futures.

While statistics can numb, they also can instruct.

● *Who's Who Among American High School Students* says one-fourth of those considered to be among the brightest students in the country have considered committing suicide; more than 20 percent have witnessed school violence; 80 percent admitted to cheating, and 15 percent said they were prejudiced against blacks and Hispanics. *Boston Globe*

● Research suggests that the increase in juvenile homicide since the 1980s is due to the fact that juveniles have more access to handguns. *New York Times*

● Narrowing the gender gap is not necessarily completely positive. While girls now perform equal to boys in math and have significantly narrowed the gap in science, they also are now smoking, drinking, and using drugs as often as boys. And while girls are still less likely to be arrested for violent crimes, the rate at which they are being arrested for such crimes is increasing faster than the rate for boys. *Washington Post*

● *The Centers for Disease Control and Prevention* report many teens are putting themselves in jeopardy, particularly with sexually transmitted diseases and gun violence. One of five teens is armed and almost one half are sexually active—seven percent before the age of 13. CNN

● Heroin use among teens, who often mistakenly think sniffing heroin is less addictive than injecting it, doubled in the first half of the '90s. *New York Times*

● Research at Baylor College of Medicine, Houston, concluded that 20 percent of children in long-term stepfamilies experience more behavioral problems than other children. The research highlighted a "boomerang" effect with families that appeared to be happy when the

children were five to seven years old, experiencing serious behavioral problems when they reached adolescence. *USA Today*
● Most teens have lied and cheated, according to the *Johnson Institute for Ethics.* Just under 50 percent of high school students admit to stealing, 70 percent admit to cheating on an exam and 92 percent have lied to their parents. *USA Today*
● The National Violence Against Women survey reports nearly 18 percent of women in the United States have been raped or the victim of attempted rape. Most were younger than 17 when they were first raped. Three-fourths of the women raped as adults said they knew the perpetrators. *Chicago Sun Times*
● *The American Society of Pediatrics* advises parents to find out whether their child's friends' houses have guns in them before letting them play there. An estimated one in three households has a gun and nearly half of all gun injuries happen in or around the home. More than 40 percent of households with children ages three to 17 have guns. *Milwaukee Journal Sentinel*

Adolescence is a time of physical and emotional turmoil. Children of this age naturally seek more independence and experiment more boldly. But it is precisely at this phase that parental involvement in the children's school activities and lives drops off. Drive by the youth soccer field some Saturday. There will be almost twice as many adults watching as there are six-year-olds playing. But check out the Under 14 games—at best, just a handful of parents.

If I can play pharmacist, I give you what the "doctors" at the Carnegie Council on Adolescent Development prescribe as good medicine for New Millennium Families:
1) Educational institutions should create schools better suited to the developmental needs of adolescents.
2) Parents should re-engage themselves with their children, with the help of more family-friendly policies by employers.
3) Health professionals should increase their efforts to educate and treat adolescents.
4) Youth organizations should expand and multiply to reach out to the one-third of adolescents who are now largely ignored.
5) The media should show more responsibility by discouraging—not glamorizing—violence, sex, and drugs.

Listen through the noise for cries

Nicky: tossed between family and foster care whenever his drug-addicted mother collapsed on another binge.

Christy: beaten and abused.

Various: one of 14 children of an addicted mother and a father too old to care for the kids.

Sandra: poor, one of many siblings who crept from apartment to apartment trying to stay ahead of the landlord.

Chris: star athlete, unmanaged, given only vague guidelines, and introduced to drugs and alcohol by his parents.

These alumni, and every one of the nearly 2,000 children Baptist Children's Homes serves annually, have their own story. They all have unique issues from yesterday that they must deal with today and tomorrow.

Their experiences cover the panorama of pain, a canvas of abuse, neglect, problems with authority and substances, poverty, homelessness, and the deaths of parents. But if there is any one umbrella issue that describes the problems of the widest slice of children in our care, it would be that they are unmanaged. An "unmanaged" child has no curfew; early cries for attention in the form of destructive behavior are ignored; the child shows little respect for adults or anyone in authority; his parents don't know and often don't care where he is; he is disruptive in controlled settings like a classroom.

A special group in Wake County (Raleigh, N.C.) recognized the need for adults to really listen to and hear children and to take seriously what the kids were saying. Very candidly, three groups of youngsters told adults that being a teenager is difficult, that they want more role models, and that they need to feel loved, supported, and trusted.

The discussions, which included children in Wake County's Juvenile Detention Center, youthful offenders who haven't been incarcerated, and children who are at risk of committing crimes, were part of a day-long seminar, "Exploring the Link Between Childhood Experiences and Juvenile Crime."

Children spoke while adults took notes. At least for part of the morning, children were leaders, and they had the attention of the very adults they and their peers longed for.

After listening to children talk about peer pressure to drink and take drugs or to wear the latest style of athletic shoe, the adults gathered by themselves and tried to sort out what they had heard.

They sat in small groups and discussed the children's comments. Children said they wished for better family relationships, male role models, good teachers, and more structure. One boy said his mom tells him to come home each night but doesn't give him a curfew.

Nothing was, or is, more apparent than the fact that youngsters need to know someone is looking out for them. Unfortunately, all youngsters don't have positive role models at home, especially positive male role models.

That special afternoon in Raleigh confirms findings from years of intense personal interaction I have had with teenagers. The hard exterior many teens show the world is their defense from attacks to the image they work so hard to establish.

Let me encourage adults to be patient with teens. Sometimes we want to throw up our hands and pray for the teen years to quickly pass. We promise ourselves we'll incorporate them back into life when time humanizes them.

If you do that, if you discount them and don't listen to their cries, you'll not know that they really need and want adults to reach out to them, to establish guidelines, to show they care by helping them manage their chaotic lives.

Statistics from The Children's Defense Fund in Washington, D.C., reveal starkly the difficulty teenagers face. Every day in the United States: 2,781 teenagers get pregnant; 1,234 children run away from home; 322 children are arrested for drinking and driving; 165 children are arrested for drug offenses; 7,400 children are reported abused or neglected; 2,680 children see their parents divorce; 105 babies die before their first birthday; 14 children are killed by guns.

These statistics will have changed by the time you read this; almost certainly not for the better. Each number behind the statistics represents a youth, a bright star that somehow has dimmed.

Violence—deadly violence—among youth increased dramatically and graphically in the final years of the 20th century. As the 21st century enters its infancy, it will take our best efforts and then some to make life better for our teens. It's a battle we must win, not only for the sake of the teens, but for our entire society.

These negative trends are not immutable laws of nature. They can be reversed. New Millennium Families can begin and continue that turnaround. And I know we will.

Resiliency enables kids to bounce back

Though they need and deserve adult and community assistance, children and teenagers bring something to the fight too—a strong spirit that often has been dampened but not extinguished by their life experiences.

Amy was abused and bewildered, but now she's married and a Christian missionary in Venezuela.

Jason's family frightened him, fought over him, tossed him about like a hot potato, but today he's pursuing a military and political career.

Marie had a baby before a driver's license, and now she wants to be a doctor.

Each of these children, and dozens like them, are rebounding from blows that would have knocked Joe Louis or Muhammad Ali or Mike Tyson from the ring. Every night BCH's beds are filled with children who were beaten literally and figuratively by life. Yet something within them, some flickering flame of resilience, keeps them coming back, keeps them surfacing when it seems they would surely drown.

Studies on teenage behavior have been a favorite of psychologists and sociologists for decades. Recently, the emphasis of those studies has shifted from what makes a kid "go bad" when trials weigh them down, to what helps a kid prosper despite those trials. Adults who "make it" after teenage turmoil clung to faith in themselves. They focused on goals and envisioned a better life. They reached out to adults, in and outside their families, who valued them.

They persevered—perhaps even grew stronger through their trials and tribulations—while others who faced the same challenges did not. The difference? We want to know. Increasingly children's advocates want to understand what fosters this ability to bounce back from adversity. We want to identify internal strengths and external supports that help at-risk children beat the odds so we can expand and multiply those factors.

Certain traits have been associated with children's resilience:

- Good intellectual skills
- A sense of self-worth
- A sense of humor
- An easygoing temperament
- A positive relationship with at least one adult

"Why study the bad kids?" is a legitimate question. "Why not study the kids who make it out of similar environments? What did they have? Put that in a program and give booster shots to kids who need that booster shot."

We know what some of those booster shots are: a mentoring adult who helps lift a child over hurdles; a deep faith that gives hope and a reason to persevere; positive role models; and a place to live where they feel safe.

New Millennium Families will thrive when they discover this antidote to failure, this booster shot to success. And it's not just for children and youth. Adults also want to apply the lessons of resilience to their daily lives. Consider the popularity of such books as *Simple Abundance* and its sequels and the enormous popularity of the *Chicken Soup for the Soul* series.

One influential resilience study, on the Hawaiian Island of Kauai, identified about 240 high-risk children, born into stress, poverty, and family conflict. Investigators followed the group's development from 1955 to 1995 and found that while two-thirds got involved in crime or developed mental problems, one-third became competent, confident, caring adults.

The resilient tended to be affectionate, outgoing, and able to recruit others to help them. They weren't always the smartest, but they communicated well and had good reading skills. They had interests and talents—intellectual, artistic, athletic—that helped them make friends, gain self-esteem, and develop a sense of purpose.

A big key is that those young people received a lot of help. They had a supportive extended family and teachers and other community members who mentored them. They were often asked to help other members of their family, such as younger siblings, instilling in them a sense of responsibility.

Compared to their troubled peers and even those who grew up in secure environments, the resilient had the highest proportion of stable marriages and the lowest proportion of unemployment, divorces, and serious health problems.

To soar above the winds of change, strong families will promote resilience. They will help children and other family members to bounce back from the blows they've absorbed. New Millennium Families will not be willing to leave anyone lying on the mat.

Chapter Five

The dawning (knowledge) of death:
Helping children—of any age—accept,
mourn and move beyond the loss of life

Death is strange—
A great range.
Death is peace—
Or quiet, at least.
Life can only be what you make it.
Death is how you treat life.
                    Jennifer, BCH child

What is death to a caterpillar
is life to a butterfly.
                    —Anonymous

Weeping may endure for a night,
but joy comes in the morning
—Psalms 30:5

Have courage for the great
sorrow of life and patience
for the small one . . . go to
sleep in peace, God is awake
                    —Victor Hugo

Emotionally unhealthy environments leave many children on shaky emotional ground to deal with such issues of death. Children face death daily—dead bugs, worms, birds, mosquitoes, flies, frogs, turtles, hamsters, dogs, cats, and gerbils.

Our family's most significant loss of a pet came when Purvis, our 18-year-old "stray kitten," had to be put to sleep. Each family member took a turn at saying good-bye and holding her before relinquishing her to the vet. This gave our son and daughter permission to grieve, an environment where it was safe to grieve and acknowledge that adulthood is no escape from sorrow.

It didn't lessen the pain when their grandparents died, but it helped them learn to deal with emotional loss in a healthy way.

Because death is so common for a child, he might pay little attention to it, except when death affects his own life.

Accepting death never is easy. The only grandparent I ever knew died of throat cancer when I was 16. My family was so caught up in the grief process—which included a sizable dose of denial—that I never verbalized my own feelings of loss. Not until I was 28 and made an intentional journey with a friend and counselor to stand beside my grandmother's grave and cry, was I able to say a few personal words to express to her my gratitude for her being a terrific grandma.

My personal experience illustrates the basic ingredient in helping a child in times of death: listen to his expressed feelings and assure him that he is not alone in his thoughts.

A child's greatest fear is fear of abandonment. He can sustain the loss that death brings if he thinks the same thing is not going to happen to him—or you.

Yet we may avoid helping children in times of death because we don't know what to say or how to act. A deeper problem is that we may not have come to grips with our own thoughts about death and dying. As in any crisis, the important thing is for the adult to "be there" for the child. The thought of a parent dying, for instance, is life threatening to a child. His first natural question is, "Am I going to be taken care of?"

That craving for security isn't bound by time or limited to food and shelter.

I know a young man with a cum laude college degree, a glittering resume, a promising career, and a wife with a good professional career of her own. He has investments and savings. He has no irrational fear that he will starve or die of exposure when his parents die.

Yet when told his mother faced a possible fatal illness, he hung up the phone and wept intermittently for hours, "because I was afraid she would not live to be grandmother to my children or see me reach my life's goals." Those who lost parents while they were still young adults know exactly what he was feeling.

You need to think about your own initial experience with death. What is your earliest memory of death and how did it affect you? Do you still feel anxious when thinking of it? Then ask, is this the kind of memory that I want this child to carry into adulthood?

Losing parents hides boundary markers

Such introspection is often complicated because we won't give ourselves permission to embrace the painful realities of death. We smile at the old joke about the man who killed both parents then pleaded for mercy because he was an orphan. Although logically absurd, doesn't part of us also reject the idea that an adult could claim the status of "orphan," no matter how his parents died?

We don't think of orphans as adults. We think of orphans as small, helpless children, and it is upon them our mercies fall. What is more touching than Oliver Twist pleading with his mean headmaster for another bowl of gruel? A young child with no parents is like a young rabbit in the woods who can't find its shelter. Every fox and hawk in the forest is looking for a way to swoop down onto that helpless creature and make a meal of it.

Realizing that I am now an orphan, I identify with the little rabbit. Not that I feel threatened by the forest wolves, but with the passing of both my parents, both my in-laws, and all of my grandparents, aunts and uncles, there is a sense that all is not as it should be back at the rabbit hole. When the person who always prayed before Thanksgiving dinner is gone, it is hard for anyone else to fill the silence; when the person who always laughed hardest at your lame jokes is silent, you struggle to find humor in anything at all.

I'm not alone in my evaluation that my generation, and especially the Baby Boomers just behind me, are not psychologically prepared for orphanhood. More and more boomers are discovering that when their parents die, bonds of memory and tradition that held their extended families together go with them. Together we are living the truth that "the only thing more difficult than having aging parents is not having aging parents." And for a youth-oriented generation conditioned to believe that modern medicine can cure or hold at bay almost every ailment, orphanhood has unwelcome, even terrifying, connotations of aging and mortality.

I buried my mother on February 9, 1996, her 83rd birthday. February 9 always was the biggest day of the year for Mom. She loved birthdays, and it was fitting that 300 of her closest friends showed up on that birthday to say good-bye. I will always believe that's the way Mother wanted it to be—and she usually got her way.

An early morning call from her nursing home alerted me that Mother's kidneys were shutting down. When the nurse handed her the phone, we shared an emotional and very loving conversation, telling each other that we loved one another very much.

As my wife, Catherine, and I made the trip from Thomasville to Asheville, my mother issued the nurses one of her famous directives: "I want you to wash my hair and put on my make-up. I will then see Mickey and will get ready to die tonight." (Mickey is my nickname. I am an only child.)

The nurses could hardly believe what they heard. "But, Mrs. Blackwell," they protested, "it will be painful for you to have your hair washed. You gained 20 pounds from fluid build-up last night and it will be very difficult to do what you ask."

Of course, Mother won out. When we arrived after the three-hour drive, she could barely speak but she sat up in bed with her silver hair, freshly washed and set, shining.

I told her how beautiful she looked, especially her hair. She smiled, called Catherine over to whisper a few unintelligible words and soon eased into unconsciousness. For several hours I held her hand, stroking her arm and patting her hand.

We had told each other our deepest feelings over the phone and shared a few light-hearted moments on my arrival when I complimented her beauty. But as those final, silent minutes passed, God granted me the opportunity to relive the complex interactions between a mother and a son. Understanding ebbed and flowed between my fingers and her skin. We celebrated, grieved, explained, and affirmed without words. It was a holy time as two of God's children wrapped up their earthly relationship.

Then, after several hours, she suddenly pulled away from my grasp. Our final conversation was over. It was time for her to break both my physical hold on her hand and the spiritual hold this world had on her body.

There was no "death rattle," just the slow ebbing of a determined life which "passed to the other side" shortly after midnight. Mother's last wish was her final gift to me and one that remains fresh and precious to this very minute: "I want to wash my hair, see Mickey, and then die."

When my time comes, I wouldn't mind going out that way and leaving my wife and children and friends such a sterling parting legacy.

I'm not alone among mid-life people who lose their parents. We often are surprised to discover we feel pretty lost and abandoned, too. We feel a rupture of connective tissue and a sense that our family is shrinking.

Compounding the loss of a parent, and the rootlessness of contemporary families, is the fact that people are now having children later than did previous generations. One result is that boomers (those born between 1946 and 1964) often lose elderly parents just when their life experience and practical advice would be most valued. And more and more children are growing up never really knowing the kindly but authoritative presence of a grandparent.

Even the physical decline of an elderly parent, which usually means surrendering the role as head of the family, can be traumatic for offspring. Coping with the day-to-day needs of their own children while also addressing the concerns of aging and infirm parents is a mid-life crisis few of us anticipate or are comfortable with. The initial decade of the new millennium will be especially challenging to the first wave of the baby boom generation.

Sometimes, the crises involving the deterioration and death of elderly parents can also have a positive, renewing effect on families. For example, caring emotionally and physically for them in their final years can unite—at least temporarily—dispersed and disparate family members. And their deaths can often induce a sense of responsibility toward the family's next generation.

Summer 1998 provided both trauma and redemption for me in this regard. My in-laws died within weeks of one another. That meant Catherine lost not only both parents close together but our children also lost their last two remaining grandparents, grandparents they were extremely close to, just as suddenly.

At that time our son, Michael Jr., was living in Charlotte with his grandmother (Grammer) while PawPaw, who had no cognitive ability, lived in a nearby nursing home. Life seemed to be progressing normally. Because my work had taken me "on the road" for several days, Michael had decided to come to Thomasville to spend the night with his mother.

At 9 p.m. he and Catherine had a delightful half-hour conversation with Grammer. There was no hint of trouble, but when Michael returned to Charlotte the next morning, he discovered his grandmother's cold, lifeless body in the kitchen.

The fall had blackened one side of her face; we surmised she died before hitting the floor. Encountering the manner and suddenness of the death was a severe shock to Michael.

Over the previous months he and Grammer had established an incredible bond of love and loyalty. Both night owls, their shared appreciation for the Atlanta Braves, *Matlock*, and *Walker, Texas Ranger* gave them an excuse to stay up to 2 a.m. night after night. But it was their discussions that made those midnight hours magical.

No subject was taboo for these soul mates—Michael's taste in music, Grammer's preference in magazines included. Her death stunned, shocked, and saddened all of us. Michael was devastated.

A couple of weeks later, my father-in-law, whom we all expected to die first, was buried beside his wife. Because of his deteriorating health, we had held Grammer's ashes, so I had the privilege and honor of conducting the joint committal service in a quaint, open-country church cemetery in the North Carolina foothills.

Because Catherine's sister lives in Virginia and her brother in Colorado, we used every means available—e-mail, phone, fax, etc.— to grieve with and support each other and stay in touch as crucial decisions were made.

Relying on technology to unite a family might seem like a poor substitute for the real thing. However, family support experts say that the important thing is to take the initiative and cope with loss and loneliness with whatever resources are at hand.

And while we battle through our emotions, children watch.

Children under ages three or four have little idea of the meaning of death. Yet, there is an emotional vacuum, particularly in the death of a parent. What better way to teach that "God is love" than to fill the emotional cavity left by a parent's death?

Children from ages four to seven often view death in biological terms. They try to understand what has happened in relationship to themselves. These children ask direct questions and should be given simple, honest answers. Try to get "inside" their experience, rather than offering trite answers.

Children from ages eight to 12 are concerned about the social meaning of death. Their questions deal with human interdependence and the breakdown of relationships when death intervenes.

Teenagers begin to form a more mature concept of death, but they also have to deal with another form of death that younger children seldom face, and that is the self-inflicted death of a friend.

Teen suicide is a national phenomenon that has been on the increase for the past 50 years. Suicide is the third leading cause of death of young people ages 15-24. Teenagers tend to see their problems as unique—to feel helpless and not in control of their lives. It is a time when young people struggle to balance the desires and capacities of adults with their own status as neither adult nor child.

I spoke at a high school baccalaureate service the night after a member of the graduating class had died of a self-inflicted gunshot wound. I discarded my manuscript and tried to help the stunned classmates deal with their shock and grief.

If you know a teenager who displays unusual moodiness, belligerence, apathy, poor eye contact, and lack of attention to hygiene, it may be time to take action. Such behavior can be a signal of suicidal tendencies.

Dealing with questions, thoughts and feelings

Rather than offer quick and easy answers when a child asks about death, try to understand the child's frame of reference. What is the child emotionally capable of handling? Remember that the tone of your voice is extremely important. The child may not remember what you tell him, but he will remember the way in which it was told. If your voice is harsh, strained, or hysterical, the child senses not only that you are uncomfortable answering his questions, but that maybe there's something else you are not telling him.

Adults also need constantly to re-examine their own ideas about death, especially their own mortality. If you are age 40, ask yourself how you would want a child to respond to questions about death when he is 40. You begin to implant the "age-40 answer" when the child is only 7 or 9 or 13.

Don't ignore children's questions. If a child wants to know "what happened to Grandpa when he died?" it is okay to say that you believe that Grandpa is in heaven. A full theological discussion of life after death isn't needed with an eight-year-old, but a simple answer provides an avenue for further discussion as the child matures.

A parent may say to his 11-year-old, "Grandfather died because he was very old and had a disease that very old people get. This probably won't happen to you or to your father and me because we are younger and expect to live for a long time."

Occasionally, a child has to deal with a sudden death. The best approach is to be straightforward: "I have some very sad news to tell you." Help the child feel secure. Let him think and reflect and ask questions.

A recurring question is whether children should attend the funeral or memorial service. Six years old is a very rough dividing line, but generally children in first grade probably should attend because it helps them understand what happened to the body. The service also may provide another opportunity for the child to share his feelings. Younger children may be left with a loving caregiver for the duration of the funeral and/or other services.

Unresolved grief

What happens to the child if he is not allowed to express his feelings of grief, anger, loss, or sadness? Unresolved grief is carried into adulthood and, ultimately, interferes with primary relationships. For instance, a seven-year-old child loses her father. Her memories are that he was strong and loving. When he died, his wife resolved to show no grief and told her child that no tears were to be shed because "Daddy would not want us to cry." The girl becomes a woman and tries to find a man to measure up to Daddy. Every man is compared to an impossible ideal. The woman finds herself avoiding intimate relationships because she is afraid she will get hurt again.

Perhaps if her feelings of grief and sorrow had been adequately dealt with when she was seven, many of her adult problems would have been avoided. Fortunately, this woman and others like her can receive help to assist them with their unresolved anxieties.

Children also may experience depression if they continue to feel abandoned and alone. Depression knows no age limit, and children as young as age four may show depressive symptoms. Depression often is a result of anger turned inward. A child can become angry because a friend or close relative has died. If those feelings are put down or ridiculed, the child may feel that anger is an out-of-bounds emotion and that he is not supposed to feel that way.

Helping children in times of death is a demanding and often draining task. But children need to see that death is a part of life, and life should be lived to its fullest.

Chapter Six

Making marriage magnificent:
Care and maintenance
of society's cornerstone

There is nothing nobler or more admirable
than when two people who see eye-to-eye
keep house as man and wife,
confounding their enemies
and delighting their friends.
> —*The Odyssey of Homer*

Marriage is more
than four bare legs in a bed.
> —*Hoshang N. Akhtar*

I married the first man I ever kissed.
When I tell this to my children they just about throw up.
> —*Barbara Bush, former First Lady*

Mark Twain may have been a great writer and humorist but he wasn't worth a crippled frog in Calavaras County as a theologian—or marriage counselor. Twain suggested that God's joke on the human race was "requiring men and women live together in marriage." Better he should have observed that humankind has made a joke out of the greatest opportunity family and society have for joy and happiness.

With few exceptions, all weddings are happy. It is the marriages that get tough. Men and women, young and old, enter marriage with such high hopes, expecting fully to overcome all the mundane realities of daily living with a blissful, dreamlike walk into the sunset.

Then reality breaks their bubbles and they flock to ministers' or therapists' offices hurt, angry, and bewildered—or else they run home to their parents or run off with a co-worker.

Go into any bookstore and check out the "marriage" section. You'll find stacks of variations on *Marriage for Dummies* or *The Idiot's Guide to a Successful Family* (even if those actual titles don't exist). Fortunately many of the volumes work from a solid Christian framework.

It may surprise you to learn, however, that guidelines for a New Millennium marriage that can be applied directly from scripture are rare. Jesus never made family relationships the theme of any major address recorded in the Gospels. Both the founder of our faith, Jesus, and its greatest interpreter, the Apostle Paul, were unmarried.

The pattern of the Biblical family does not provide a great deal of help. Frankly, the big names of the Old Testament are not examples of family virtue. Most of these Hebrew heroes had more than one marriage going at one time. Abraham had Sarah and Hagar. David started out with six wives and quickly expanded the number of wives and mistresses. Solomon accumulated 700 wives and 300 mistresses. And all of them had times of what today would be called "dysfunctional."

By New Testament times people had figured out that God meant it when he ordained a one man-woman marriage until death did them part. But specifics on family living are scarce.

Therefore it is up to us to take the great principles of our faith and apply them to our domestic arrangements. Jesus' Golden Rule—"Do unto others as you would have them do unto you"— is a relevant application and his words on forgiveness always apply.

Paul's classic words in *I Corinthians 13* speak directly to our modern scene: "Love is patient and kind . . . Love does not insist on its own way . . . Love keeps no score of wrongs . . ." His further instruction to focus on "whatever is true . . . honorable . . . just . . . pure . . . lovely" is worth a second reading for our personal relationships.

Conceding that even the best marriages experience turmoil, let me give you some common sense suggestions, not pearls of wisdom from one who knows all the answers, but from a fellow struggler who fusses and gets fussed at just like the rest of you.

Realize that in your marriage neither of you should dominate the other. Marriages should be equal opportunity arrangements. Marriage is not an obedience test. Lasting happiness can be achieved only as each partner regards the other as an intelligent, unique individual and each allows the other to become the complete person he or she was intended to be. The Bible clearly speaks of proper and mutual respect within marriage.

Learn to negotiate. As Paul said, "Love does not insist on its own way." Most every disagreement can be negotiated. You have to be honest, up-front, and conciliatory. You can't demand you be the "winner" every time. You can't threaten to take your marbles and go home—you already are home! You don't have to understand everything your spouse does or thinks—but you need to accept the individual differences that don't damage the marriage. (Later in this chapter we will spend a lot more time looking at the role communication plays in marriage, especially the negotiation segment.)

Look for new ways to do joyful things together. Although the blazing romance may not be the same as it was 30 years ago, the bond can be stronger than ever before. It means you have to be creative and interesting—and not so tied up with your children that you neglect your own relationship. Remember, your connections need to last long after your offspring leave home—and if you're tied to someone, it is a lot more enjoyable if you enjoy them.

Eliminate the little irritants that get on the other's nerves. Little things can be annoying. Find out what bugs her and work to exterminate it—or at least tone it down.

We talk about a husband "suddenly" asking for a divorce or a wife "suddenly" being attracted to a co-worker and having an affair. But there is no such thing as "suddenly" in an intimate partnership like marriage. People who are surprised have neglected to see the signposts along the route and failed to deal constructively with day-to-day challenges.

Emphasize the positive qualities of your marriage. The good qualities may outnumber the bad 10-1, but we usually focus on the "ugly." Consciously remain aware of all the positives about your spouse and your marriage. Accent the strengths you see. Offer praise and offer it generously. Be upbeat. Keep yourself attractive.

And learn that when an issue is over, it's over. Ogden Nash's on-target advice to husbands also rings true for wives:

> To keep your marriage brimming
> With love in the loving cup
> Whenever you're wrong, admit it.
> Whenever you're right, shut up.

Anyone who has done much marriage counseling realizes that most people asking for advice are unclear if they want to stay in the marriage or get out. But they do know that "status quo" has to translate into "status go." Pain and frustration outweigh any value they see in continuing the relationship in its current condition. Only the most courageous of couples choose to take what they have and rebuild a relationship they can thrive in.

Have you noticed that popular culture speaks of "falling out of love" as the natural reversal of "fall in love?" Yet we speak of "walking out" on a marriage or a family! We deceive ourselves in the first instance because if it really is love, you "walk out of love" too. Falling is an accident, something that happens to us, mostly out of our control. Walking, however, is a conscious act, putting one foot in front of another in a purposeful direction.

It is much easier to fall into something than to fall out of it. You can fall into a well or a vat of oatmeal but you don't fall out—once you're "committed" by the fall, it takes intentional effort to reverse the situation. Admittedly, you can fall out of an airplane or a roller coaster, but you didn't fall into them to start with!

I readily concede that American culture provides lots of ways to "fall" into what we too lightly call love. But routes for walking out of love, though invitingly wide, are few in number.

Because, I believe, even more than loud arguments or passive inattention, real indicators of marriages in trouble are chronic criticism, contempt, defensiveness, and emotional withdrawal. These destructive behaviors often lead to what psychologists call "flooding," when spouses are so overwhelmed by negative emotions that their heart rates rise, skin becomes clammy, and emotions hijack the more rational side of their brains.

The good news is that these patterns can be changed once spouses recognize the role each plays in creating them and learn how to communicate more effectively—and the earlier in the relationship the better. The bad news is that the people most needful of dealing with their destructive behaviors are the least likely to seek help or even admit the problems exist. Young couples buy into the myth that successful marriage is the effortless norm and fear social censure if they are seen as failures.

Nothing could be further from the truth.

To succeed in an institution increasingly besieged by the pressures of dual careers, changing gender roles, withering communication ties, and the torrent of misinformation on TV sitcoms, couples must work hard to develop a style of interaction that works for both. Very often, husbands and wives bring very different styles of communication to the marriage—patterns learned from their families and deeply ingrained.

Since men and women first started saying, "I do," and then discovered they really didn't, social scientists and ministers alike have been trying to quantify elements that predict a successful marriage.

At the same time, they've tried to identify predictors of marriage failure. By so doing, they hope to help young couples avoid bad matches, and help married people spot trouble early, to begin taking "evasive measures" to avoid a marriage crash.

Some returns are now in. And you may be surprised two ways.

First, lamp-throwing, glass-breaking, threat-shouting couples may not be the ones most likely to divorce. But neither are their opposites, couples who agree to avoid conflict and live passively.

The most likely to dissolve? Those that exhibit the four chronic behaviors I mentioned earlier: criticism, contempt, defensiveness, and withdrawal.

Numerous researchers, including psychologist John Gottman who calls the behaviors "the four horsemen of the apocalypse," designate them as the strongest predictors of separation and divorce. Everything in my personal experience and professional training agrees.

It's not the amount of empathy or understanding in a relationship that primarily predicts who is going to make it and who is going to divorce. Those "four horsemen" of negative behavior patterns are far more predictive. Two decades ago we were told that to maintain a healthy self-esteem, a child needed daily to hear seven compliments. We might quibble about the exact number (as if it were important!) but the basic truth is solid. We hear the negative much more loudly and ponder it much longer and more deeply while we tend to discount the positives.

If that is true for us individually and in relation to our children, why wouldn't it apply to marriage? When another competitive driver full of "road rage" calls me a jerk, so what? But if my wife accuses me with the same word or even the same tone of voice, it activates alarms. Or I can pile up a couple of dozen "sparkles" for our marriage with simple compliments or cleaning out the bathtub or watching *Wheel of Fortune* instead of the evening news—but a single put-down bankrupts that emotional account.

Basically anger and disagreement by themselves are not harmful to a marriage; it's when that anger is blended with contempt and defensiveness that it's very destructive. Jesus didn't say, "Never raise your voice;" he said, "Be angry but sin not." Another New Testament passage advises: "Let not the sun go down on your wrath." In other words, "deal with it and move on."

While much of previous marriage research has been anecdotal and sometimes contradictory, the newest findings are unusually consistent and reflect emerging insights.

Many researchers, for example, agree that it is typically the wife who takes emotional responsibility for the status of the marriage. She is most often the one who brings up the thorny issues that need to be negotiated and resolved if the marriage is to succeed, and she is the one who persists until the discussion ends in a satisfactory resolution—or a screaming match.

When the wife gives up the role of emotional caretaker and withdraws, typically after years of destructive conflict, many marriages hit rock bottom.

Husbands, and men in general, are much more uncomfortable with conflict in relationships and thus more likely to withdraw from a potential argument, either by placating their wives, even though they might be steaming inside, or by stonewalling—becoming silent and disengaged. The husband who turns on the television or walks out of the room is typical of this scenario.

Such action on a one-time or rare basis may just be an appropriate way to let the situation cool off before it is discussed. But a regular pattern of withdrawal or stonewalling by the husband is strongly predictive of divorce. Conversely, constant criticism or contempt on the part of the wife is also predictive of marital distress and divorce. It often leads to a vicious cycle. The wife criticizes or blames the husband, the husband becomes defensive and either withdraws from the discussion or defends himself by going on the attack. The result is a highly destructive fight that can end in verbal or even physical abuse.

Or it can end in the sound of nothing. Silence fills the communication channels. Have you noticed how many problems are accompanied by communication breakdowns?

War explodes when negotiations end (Winston Churchill's famous dictum: "It's better to 'jaw-jaw' than 'war-war.'"). Lost radio contact precedes most plane crashes; when phones "go dead," so does conversation; when computer links fail, so does the exchange of information.

Likewise, wives and husbands who allow their communication channels to clog, or who never open such channels, own a marriage license in serious trouble of expiring.

The problem, proclaims a nearly unanimous consensus, results from differing basic communication styles.

The earlier analogies hold. When one side thinks in Russian and the other in Chinese—and both speak through interpreters—the odds of talking out sensitive issues rapidly become remote. If static drowns out seven words out of ten, the air traffic controller and the pilot have problems understanding each other. Computers built on different technological platforms can't "speak" directly to each other.

Generally, men talk to convey information and to solve problems, whether the problem is how to finance a new car or decide who is the greatest college running back of all time. Women talk to express emotions and feelings. They talk to "connect" while men talk to "fix."

Whatever the situation in your marriage, work on communication, verbal and non-verbal. There are many good books and Christian marriage retreats that can help.

When you feel communication shutting down, remember one of my favorite cartoons. A husband and wife sit at the breakfast table, drinking coffee. The woman is thinking, "Our marriage is in trouble, we better talk about it." The man is thinking, "Our marriage is in trouble, I better keep my mouth shut."

Learning to communicate successfully lets a couple deal with clear issues in mutually understandable ways. Study after study show couples need to tell each other how they feel and that such kind honesty cements matrimony.

To me, modern research has again confirmed the ancient biblical wisdom of men and women loving and serving their spouses.

I am encouraged that, for most of us, there are specific, concrete things we can look at and work on to free-up our marriages to practically unlimited happiness and passages of joy. Marital distress comes only in a few forms, even though those forms are big and tough and ugly. But marital happiness comes packaged in more flavors than Baskin-Robbins could ever imagine.

Remember those four horsemen: criticism, contempt, defensiveness, and withdrawal? Tame them and you can ride like the wind and on the wind—together.

The Church and divorce

But what about the horses that won't be broken, the problems that break the marriage before you and/or your spouse can break free from the destructive patterns?

It's a problem that almost defies solution. Books have been written about "painless divorce" and "creative divorce." Don't believe them. Divorce is painful. It takes an emotional toll not only on the husband and wife, but on children, parents, family, and friends. "Painless divorce" is a myth.

Churches haven't always known how to affirm the divorced person. She's been ignored, excluded, and misunderstood. He's been prohibited from teaching Sunday School or holding office. They've been morally judged, socially nudged, and spiritually budged. Some divorced persons feel like non-persons in their church as they move from the Couples Bible Study Class to the Singles Class.

They don't feel good about themselves. Whether they sought the split or not, most of them experience guilt, depression, and remorse. Feelings of failure are common. Thoughts of suicide creep in. There is pressure to reconcile, give in, and try again. "It's obviously his fault," the wife's father intones as families of the divorced couple choose sides. "If she had just paid him a little more attention, this would never have happened," the husband's mother retorts.

The Church cannot ignore the problem if it is to remain The Church. Thankfully, many congregations have begun creative ministries for the divorced. Others want to be a part of the solution but don't know how.

A church's own tradition may keep it from doing anything. A divorced person may move to another church because his or her needs aren't being met.

Divorce recovery seminars have become quite popular. Resistance to them has eased. Churches are recognizing that divorced people have unique needs: self-esteem has been damaged and self-worth questioned. There also is the problem of re-entry into the world of dating or relationship building.

With more and more divorces occurring after 30 years of marriage, churches are having not only to deal with the pain of divorce, but with problems accompanying other mid-life crises.

So what is the local church to do? Certainly it cannot bury its head and pretend problems don't exist. Thankfully, few churches take this approach. The church's response to divorce must be gracious, creative, cautious, redemptive, spiritual, and affirming.

First, the church must not ignore the situation. Divorce is a fact of life. The church, born in the midst of pain and persecution, must not ignore those whose pain is real. The insecurity and sense of loss that some divorced persons feel will not automatically go away on its own. The church's ministry to the divorced must be grace-filled. It must speak to the uniqueness of God's love. It must offer forgiveness and acceptance.

Second, the church must provide avenues for redemption. Whether it's a divorce recovery class, or a weekend retreat, or a class composed mostly of divorced persons, the church can find ways to say, "We care."

Third, the church must minister to the emotional hurts of the divorced person. Such competence is lacking in many churches because professional staff often do not have adequate counseling skills. Even so, staff should know how to refer the divorced person to someone who can help.

Fourth, churches should include the divorced persons in positions of responsibility. To reject someone who is already feeling rejected is painful at best, sinful at worst. Divorced people are God's children, too. They laugh, cry, hurt, rejoice, and have talents just like everyone else.

The scriptural ideal is for husbands and wives to remain together until death. If unbearable circumstances do lead to divorce, the church must remain constant in its witness, compassionate in its outreach, and creative in its redemptive ministry.

Divorce does defy easy solution. The Church, under the power of God, must become part of the answer, not part of the problem.

Marriage failures assault children

One of the most destructive ways children are put at risk becomes clearer every day. They are endangered because the institution of marriage is being driven to its knees, weakened by the abuse of a generation for whom commitment is a curse. Like a wildebeest cut off from the herd by hungry lions, marriage has withstood charge after charge, but its head is drooping and its knees grow weak.

The Council on Families in America suggests this generation of children could be "the first in our nation's history to be less well-off—psychologically, socially, economically, and morally—than their parents were at the same age." Child well-being is deteriorating, as reflected in statistics on everything from poverty and substance abuse to depression, homicide, and suicide. The council blames that deterioration on the failure of "the divorce revolution" which has led to the "weakening of marriage as an institution."

With marriage commitment weak, divorce is at an historic high and unwed parenthood has soared. Children are the principal victims.

Some earlier proponents of making divorce easier are rethinking that position. For most the idea behind simplifying the legal ritual of divorce was not to produce more divorces but to make it easier for someone to escape a disastrous marriage. If "disastrous" is an accurate description, I believe the same thing.

Those instincts were right, but now America is in the throes of unintended consequences. A weakened marital commitment may best be captured by the phrase inserted into many modern wedding vows: "so long as we both shall love." I know of couples who pose for "divorce portraits" so they can display them on the coffee table alongside their wedding album—a sort of before and after study in still life.

Consider some of the reasons 100,000 respondents to a national survey gave for getting a divorce. The results were published in *The Day America Told the Truth—What People Really Believe About Everything That Really Matters.*

- Communication problems-64%
- Spouse was not faithful-58%
- Constant fighting-58%
- Emotional abuse-52%
- Falling out of love with spouse-49%
- Unsatisfactory sex-45%
- Spouse didn't make enough money-31%
- Physical abuse-28%
- Falling in love with someone else-22%
- Boredom-22%

Respondents could select multiple reasons, but one in five said boredom was a reason to get divorced! No wonder children suffer with that level of commitment from parents.

The "no fault" divorce movement laid out such worthy goals: to foster greater equality between men and women, to improve the family lives of women, and to expand individual happiness and choice. But "no fault" wasn't the same as "no victim." Society forgot to ask children about the pain of being severed from a mother or a father and factor it into the equation.

Hasn't the result been a decrease in individual happiness, along with growing economic insecurity for women and increased isolation for men? For children, hasn't the result been an increase of sadness, neglect, and rage?

As president of BCH, an organization that deals daily with hundreds of children victimized by parental non-commitment, as a husband and father of two, I agree that marriage as a stable cornerstone of society is being driven to its knees. Far too often children are pinned beneath those knees and ground into the dirt.

I resoundingly affirm every effort by churches, communities, families, ministers, peers, friends, bosses, co-workers, and individuals to support, uplift, rescue, renew, and recommit to marriage as society's bedrock and specifically to their spouses.

Two parents are kids' best hope

I've always known that a child is better off being raised in a household with two parents. That view has been questioned by many who want to affirm parents who have made the decision to split up, and by others who feel children are better off with a single parent than in a quarrelsome household.

I also know that growing up in a two-parent family is not automatic bliss for every child today. And no one has to tell me about single parents doing a tremendous job. The depth of satisfaction I feel when BCH is allowed to help a single parent regain control of his or her life and reunite parent and child in a healthy home can't be measured. Neither can the respect I feel for them.

But I have felt for years that any child has a better chance of a bright future if his or her parents are able to work hard enough, and successfully enough, at their own relationship to stay together.

Scholarly research backs up my instincts: a child's best protection against becoming a single parent, dropping out of school, using drugs, or living in poverty is to be raised in a two-parent family.

In the late 1950s, 95 percent of young children were growing up with two married parents. Today, less than 60 percent of young children are growing up with two married parents.

The research demonstrates in objective terms the many ways children raised in single-parent homes are at greater risk throughout their lives: of becoming single parents themselves, of living in poverty, of becoming teenage parents, of dropping out of high school or college, of using drugs.

Children need a supervisory shield that only parents can provide. It's hard work and two parents can better provide such a shield.

Children copy their models. You know how hard it is to tell your child not to smoke if you smoke. Children raised in a negative lifestyle find it difficult to turn away from it—and few do. A negative lifestyle, instead of being rejected, is embraced as their reference point for normalcy.

Children raised in two-parent families also are least likely to use drugs. Nearly 60 percent of high school students from two-parent families report they never have used drugs, compared to 53 percent of teens raised by a single mother, 46 percent of teens raised by a single father, and 36 percent of teens raised by non-relatives.

The researchers highlight an inseparable connection between the effects of single parenthood and poverty. Each problem makes the other worse; determining which is the cause and which is the effect isn't always easy.

Compelling evidence argues that the principal producer of family poverty is divorce which results in single-parent families. Forty-three percent of women growing up in poor, one-parent families end up having children of their own while unwed.

A major distinction between two-parent families and one-parent families is the potential to have two incomes. While the percentage of single mothers in the workforce has increased only slightly since 1949, the percentage of mothers in two-parent families who are in the workforce has grown dramatically, from 10 percent in 1949 to more than 60 percent today. This will probably continue to increase in the new millennium.

Family structure and income also have a strong impact on educational issues, since young people who drop out of high school or college are more likely to have grown up in a single-parent family.

Among children raised in two-parent families, about 13 percent drop out of high school. That compares to 23 percent of children raised by a parent who remarries or by a divorced mother with custody; 36 percent raised by a divorced father with custody; and 37 percent raised by an unmarried mother.

So parents, please work hard to maintain or to rekindle the affection that brought you together. You may have to bite your tongue. You may have to sacrifice some of your individuality. You may have to delay pursuit of some individual interests while your children are at home.

But I just know your children are worth the effort.

Chapter Seven

Expending extended family:
Grandmas, grandpas,
in-laws and outlaws

Pessimists remind us that
lilies belong to the onion family,
and optimists
that onions belong to the lily family.
—*Yolaine Dippenweiler*

> *Lack of emotional security of American young people*
> *is due to isolation from the larger family unit. No*
> *mere father and mother are enough to*
> *provide emotional security for a child. He needs to*
> *feel himself one in a world of kinfolk,*
> *persons of variety in age and temperament.*
> —*Pearl S. Buck*

All your pains and cares are past,
And you're so happy and free;
Now that you're home at last,
You're much better off than me.
> *The time we spent with each other,*
> *Is so very precious to me;*
> *There will never be another grandmother,*
> *Who was loved more than thee.*
>> *I'm coming to meet you one day,*
>> *When on wings of love I fly away.*
>> *What a reunion that will be,*
>> *When you and Jesus I shall see.*
>> —*Shannon, BCH child*

What part of the traditional wedding ceremony least connects with
reality? Our discussion shows that the "love and honor" part is pretty

meaningless for lots of folks. "In sickness and in health?" Marriage to an emotional or physical invalid is more than many can sustain.

But I vote for the answer to the minister's question, "Who gives this woman to this man." This is not the time or place to discuss if the question infers that the bride is property or not. My concern is the answer: "Her mother and I."

On the surface and literal level, this declaration seemingly signifies the transfer of the woman's identity from her biological family to her husband's clan. Many cultures have ritual kidnappings where the bride's family puts up comic resistance and wails loudly as their kinswoman is dragged, kicking and screaming (and, hopefully, laughing) from her parents' home by friends and relatives of the groom.

But in America, traditionally, we make do with a question and an answer. Notice also that no one asks "Who gives this man to this woman?" No mother-of-a-mama's-boy stands up and declares: "His father and I."

The couple may leave the church to the music and words of "I only have eyes for you" but when they get around to looking around, they discover they created an intersection of two families—and the traffic runs heavy north-south as well as east-west.

A pastor acquaintance and his young bride moved a thousand miles away from their relatives to go to seminary—free from meddling in-laws. Then came the Thursday before their first weekend visit home. In the supermarket my friend happily tossed bags of cookies and chips and candy and bread and juice and soft drinks into the shopping cart. Or he *would* have put all that in the basket if he had not felt his wife's icy stare boring into the back of his head. "What are you doing?" asked an equally icy voice. "Getting snacks for the trip," he replied shakily.

Within minutes the battle was joined—loudly. A thousand miles from their parents, they fumed and sputtered with each other because, he says, "In my family we weren't even out of the city limits before my mom started slapping together peanut butter and jelly sandwiches and passing them over the seat." But her family "*never, ever* ate or drank in the car. If we wanted a soft drink or a bag of peanuts, we waited until we stopped at a service station and finished them before getting back in the car."

Another young couple met and married in their mid-30's. Both had lived away from their parents for years. They started married life in Nevada while their folks were safely in Texas. The safety evaporated the first time he decided to be helpful and do the laundry. "What are you doing?" asked a voice that seemed to be coming from the North Pole (maybe you recognize it).

Seems they had inherited different methods of sorting dirty clothes and belonged to different denominations of laundry. (By the way, I do my own laundry, thank you.)

Not much evidence of giving someone to another family is there?

So, if you're married, unless you wed a true (and multi-generational) orphan, you have in-laws. If you have children, the odds are overwhelming that you will become an in-law.

So shake off the stereotypes, deal with the realities, and work on the possibilities. Your life, your marriage, and your children will be richer for it. If you live in the ocean anyway, you have to learn to swim— so why not go ahead and learn to surf so you can enjoy it!

Here are some suggestions:

Newlyweds:

1. Remember that you didn't love her/him first and you'll never love him/her longer—parents have a 25-year head start. They may have some guilt that they can no longer protect her/him and may criticize you unfairly because of their own feelings. They may have genuine concern they have a right to express (but not harp on). Be gracious. You won. You married her/him.

2. Never forget that your primary duty as spouse is to the integrity and well-being of your marriage. If that means disappointing her parents (or his), do it gently and only if necessary. (See: "Holidays, where to spend them.").

3. Be fair to each other. The Golden Rule applies to in-laws too. Talk about stresses you feel with your in-laws, but never when you're angry. Comedian Jeff Foxworthy rightly notes that when two people are dating, they can't fight very much because they only pick on each other. But after the wedding they can attack their spouse's entire family, reaching as far as necessary to drag out bad examples.

4. Don't be a pampered guest at your in-laws unless they insist you to be—and mean it. Join in their family traditions and activities; clean up your own mess (and other folks' when you can); listen to and learn the "family stories;" leave the last piece of lemon pie for her dad or his mother.

5. Deflect criticism of your career, political preference, or choice in cars with humor and by getting to know your in-laws' positions and the reasoning behind them. Concede any points you honestly can. Don't be baited into arguments that have no productive purpose. If you're insulted, see if it was unintentional. If it wasn't, respond with dignity and restraint.

6. Ask advice and listen to it respectfully. You don't have to follow it but at least hear it. The mere act of soliciting their opinions can create bonds. And you just might learn something. Of course, if you aren't going to follow the advice, don't pretend you are.

7. Don't criticize their son/daughter in front of them or them to other people. Deal with conflicts in private and calmly. It's okay to get angry but don't lower yourself to get even.

8. When they hurt you, work through the process of forgiveness. This will benefit you, your spouse, your children, and your in-laws. When you hurt them, seek their forgiveness for the same reasons.

9. If they become enfeebled, share the responsibility of caring for them with your spouse. Treat them the way you want your husband/wife to treat your parents in the same situation.

10. Be generous in sharing your children with their grandparents. Make clear the values and boundaries that must be maintained with the children but allow the generations to love and learn from each other as often as possible.

Parents:
1. Remember that your child deserves a full, mature relationship with his/her spouse. You gave your child the confident smile and stiff backbone—but she/he produced the sparkle in the eye and the joy in the laugh. Of course your child didn't marry a person good enough for her/him. They both settled for an imperfect spouse just as they did for imperfect parents.

2.   Never forget that your child's adult potential requires severing the parent/child dependency. Of course it hurts! But it is necessary to avoid emotional paralysis. Help the process along and the remaining bonds of love will be stronger.

3.   Play fair with your daughter/son-in-law. The Golden Rule applies to them too. Talk about stresses and conflicts but never when you're angry.

4.   Their house is not your house (even if you made the down payment and provided all the furniture). Don't be a guest unless they invite you to be—and mean it. Call before you visit, give them time and space to build their own friendships. If you don't like the decor, keep it to yourself. If you can't tolerate the music or television selections, and you determine that it is something they really enjoy, read a book or magazine.

5.   Deflect criticism of your career or political preference or choice in cars with humor and by getting to know your son/daughter-in-law's views and the reasoning behind them. Concede any points you honestly can. Don't be baited into arguments that have no productive purpose. If you're insulted, see if it was unintentional. If it wasn't, respond with dignity and restraint.

6.   Offer advice in a non-threatening way and keep graciously quiet if it is refused. And always resist temptations to say, "I told you so" if the advice you offered proves correct.

7.   Don't criticize their spouse in front of them or them to other people. Deal with conflicts in private and calmly. It's okay to get angry but don't lower yourself to get even.

8.   When they hurt you, work through the process of forgiveness. Take the high road. This will benefit you, your spouse, your son/daughter, and your grandchildren. When you hurt her/him, seek his/her forgiveness for the same reasons.

9.   When they need help—financially, emotionally, physically—give it quietly and evenly and make very sure it is needed and will not hurt more than help. Be honest if you don't think you can help. You don't "owe" them anything except what Christian and parental love demands—but if you do help, do so without strings.

10. Grandchildren are not an opportunity to get revenge. Love them within the guidelines set by their parents. If you don't like the

rules, try to negotiate outside the hearing of the grandchildren. If you still don't agree to them, don't keep the grandkids. Don't criticize their parents to them, don't bribe them to win their affection, don't compete with the other grandparents.

Grandparents have special roles

We touched on the grandparent role as part of the discussion on in-laws. But the subject deserves an expanded look.

Florists and card shops provide lots of "special" days for which we are to buy gifts and offer personal remembrances. I can't keep up with them all. But one I look forward to each year is an opportunity to celebrate the special place of grandparents in our society, and in children's lives. And I'm not even a grandparent. Yet!

In an era when grandparents are increasingly the closest intact family unit a child relates to, their importance increases. How many children can say, "I would never have made it without my grandparents"? That is, in fact, what many children who are cared for by Baptist Children's Homes say. Society can't comprehend, much less repay, the debt it owes to the grandparents.

Today, 3.2 million grandparents have set aside their own plans and are raising their grandchildren, giving up their dreams of carefree final years. The trend is the result of multiple crises in American family life and has become a primary line of defense against its demise. Grandparents are closest to the fragmenting family and usually more responsive to the needs of the children that are being scarred by parents' irresponsible actions.

The modern geographical scattering of the American family often means that the grandkids have moved to Chicago or the grandparents have retired to Florida. Feeding off their own parents' left-over rebellion of the 1960s, children often see their grandparents as totally out of touch with their world. Unfortunately, grandparents often live up to that reputation.

Yet, where necessity requires grandparent-grandchild interaction or where innovation creates it, such as programs linking old with young in a foster-family setting, the potential for good things is great.

Here are some ways grandparents, biological or foster, can enhance the lives of our children and society itself:

1. Resurrect or initiate rituals, ceremonies, and gatherings. When a hit movie heightens interest in World War II or the space race, share your memories of those times. Avoid the "my generation was so much better than yours." Approach it as a chance to grant the children a legacy, a history they would otherwise not have.

A grandparent's expressed belief in the value and potential of a grandchild helps that child believe in her/himself.

2. Go multi-media. There are times, especially when children are younger, that storytelling is the best way to go. But teenagers don't often sit still for long-winded lectures. So supplement the verbal one-on-one. Organize those photos into albums and the home videos by subject and event so when someone looks at them years from now they will make sense and convey time and place. Undertake an oral history project. What religious experiences shaped you? What are your favorite books, songs, and movies? Why? What did you believe about the major issues of your day?

Let the children know these tapes exist so they can listen when they are ready. Also think about recording an emotional will for each person in your life. From the grave you can tell them you loved them and why, you can share why you were proud to be their grandparent, and challenge them to grow into the men and women God wants them to be.

3. Communicate with the grandchildren about when and where to get together and what you can do—but don't blindside the parents and don't let the grandchildren play you against their parents.

4. Forfeit your hereditary right to be a grumpy old fogey. Actually listen to the lyrics of your grandchildren's music—or have them translate if necessary—and discuss them. In your youth, didn't you join with Bob Dylan's "Blowing In the Wind" in advising adults, "don't criticize what you don't understand." Your grandchildren likely feel the same way.

5. Look around for children in your orbit who don't have access to grandparents and make yourself, your wisdom, and your love available to them. All of us frequently should ask ourselves, "What is worth doing? What will be most rewarding and yield the highest rate of enrichment to our lives?" But grandparents likely have fewer remaining years to bring fruitful answers to those questions.

Michael C. Blackwell

Grandparents help to build strong foundations, imparting values and purpose. Grandparents give grandchildren roots and wings. Celebrate Grandparent's Day year round by strengthening your family's connections to its culture, heritage, and roots.

In our mobile culture, it often takes special effort to keep children in touch with their grandparents. You might be too far away to celebrate birthdays and holidays together. While a phone call finishes a distant second to a hug, it's still a lot better than an empty space and silence. Make the effort. You'll reap rewards.

Chapter Eight

Parenting to your potential: Those vital first months key to long-term success

Life is like a puzzle
You look for the missing pieces.
It's like being in an endless garden—
You go on for ever and ever.
My life is confusing, and I don't understand it.
You go on looking for the missing piece
The piece that makes it all complete.
*   —Patricia, BCH child*

> *Parents are the bones upon which children*
> *sharpen their teeth.*
> *   —Peter Ustinov*

> *Adolescence is a period of rapid change.*
> *Between the ages of 12 and 17, for example,*
> *parents age as much as 20 years.*
> *   —Anonymous*

The first plaintive wail of a newborn child sits high atop any list of distinctive sounds, especially if the child is your own. Whether prompted by a slap to its bottom or self-generated, that wail declares, "From now on, things are going to be a little different around here."

A sensitive nurse or midwife will lay the squalling child upon its mother's chest, where it picks up the heartbeat that had been its life's cadence for the previous nine months. That heartbeat and touch comfort infants who have just emerged from the only life they have known—a warm, dark, cramped, quiet, wet, but very safe existence. The sudden thrust into a bright, dry, noisy space as big as the world stuns them.

These first moments are precious. They are both fruit and root: the fruit of long labor and the root of a lifetime relationship. It's important to begin in those early moments the bonding process that will forever link parent and child in a positive relationship. Bonding with both parents through the next six months is extraordinarily important as well, as your infant's senses come to full alert and begin to absorb the constant data stream pouring across his or her antennae.

For the last three decades, the sweetest single word I've heard is the captivating sound of "Daddy" pouring from the lips of my daughter and son. (Okay, it's been "Dad" for most of those years but I can revel in memories, can't I?) How can you make the most of those precious early months, not just so you have a wonderful time with your new baby, but so the baby's needs are met as well?

You can't spoil the child

Grandma might say differently, but you cannot "spoil" your baby in the first six months by holding it too much. An infant is not trying to manipulate you. If it's crying, it needs to be changed, is hungry, or needs to feel your loving arms. So pay attention!

An ancient English king wondered if babies were born with language skills embedded. So he put several newborn infants in isolation and decreed no one could speak to them; all physical contact was kept to an absolute minimum. He waited to see if they would speak English or German or French. They didn't speak. They died. Adequate food and shelter—without the energizing interaction with others—was not enough to sustain them.

We can throw out the evil king and look to our own history for more proof. A study of "foundling homes" in the United States in 1915 revealed that orphanages which gave babies good food and clean homes but enforced a "no coddling" policy still had almost a 100 percent mortality rate. The babies died from lack of touch.

An infant is born with a powerful need to be held. Imagine, it has just come from a constant, lifelong, warm embrace. In the womb, it cannot move without feeling its mother's body enveloping it. Touch is a silent reassurance that the baby's world is safe. The more touch, the better.

From observation at BCH's programs for infant and toddlers, I recognized that babies who were touched cried the least, even when later left alone. The message is clear: For babies to grow up to be loving, caring, affectionate, and considerate adults, they need to experience an abundance of devoted touching and cuddling. This touching not only ensures their survival, but gives them a feeling of being loved and cared for. When babies feel loved, they are able to grow in that love and give love to others—and our entire society will benefit.

Stimulating environment

Provide a stimulating environment for your infant. Their eyes and ears are huge portals, open to their world for the first time. They will be imprinted with the sights, sounds, smells, and touches they first experience.

When they awaken, it's not immediately necessary to move them from their cribs. Let them linger there, but provide something for them to "do." Do you have a brightly colored mobile they can watch dance with the air currents? Is there something in their cribs that will make a noise when they accidentally bat it with their waving, roaming hand? Eventually, they will figure out they can control that five-fingered ham at the end of their arm and make the noisemaker make the noise.

After a few months, bath time can be a wonderful time to explore the sounds and sensations of water. The "pop" when the baby's hand slaps the surface, the parent's shriek when they get splashed, the distortion of objects viewed through a layer of water. Don't rush through every bath. Put in some cups and floating toys. As you enrich your baby's cognitive skills, you'll also make some wonderful memories.

Without a stimulating environment, your infant would just lie there, looking at the ceiling or watching the neighbor's dog out the window. It's tough to get a good start on living when you're lying still.

Stimulation isn't limited to touch and sight. Don't forget hearing. Music soothes. Play music in the room when the child is awake. If you played music while pregnant, your infant will subconsciously recognize the same music played now. Your child will be comforted with the continuity of life and know that "all is well."

Baby talk

If you took seriously the notion that bonding starts even before the child is born, you probably started talking to him/her before birth. What language did you use? Do you speak "people talk" or "baby talk?" You do realize that babies don't understand the vocabulary of "baby talk" any better than they understand regular speech?

Don't confuse that eager intellect that is trying to organize all those sounds by, in essence, asking him to learn two languages simultaneously.

You needn't make up words to talk to your baby. Use regular vocabulary. Why make up words for body parts and functions? The baby is neither offended nor appeased by the words it learns as you talk in these early months.

Express your love. Your voice quality and resonance can calm and reassure the baby. And soon you will notice the baby brighten when you talk, because it will associate your loving voice with your loving actions of holding and tender care.

Share your dreams with your child, even before he/she can understand. Your easy conversation with a child in a non-threatening environment—non-threatening because he/she can't understand a word you're saying—will make it easier to talk frankly with your children as they grow, and as the issues get stickier. You are laying the groundwork for vital communication in teenage years when you establish a habit of talking to your child as an infant.

Day care

More than 60 percent of American mothers with preschool age children are in the work force. In my state of North Carolina, that number is above 75 percent.

Every working mom is faced with the decision about returning to her job after her child is born. Those who consciously adopted a lifestyle that can be supported by a single income have planned ahead and can stop working when their child is born. For those involved in a career they don't want to put on hold, and those who must return to work for economic reasons, the decision is also ready-made, but it's no easier to live with.

In 1964 Baptist Children's Homes foresaw the trend and set up a model day care center on campus so groups, especially churches, considering opening a day care could study a working model. Children are drawn from the surrounding community which welcomed it enthusiastically. The desire for quality child care and the competition for the scarce available spaces spawned a standing joke at our Fleshman-

Pratt Early Childhood Education Center. "When a Davidson County woman finds out she is pregnant, the second person she calls is her husband—right after she calls Fleshman-Pratt to get on the waiting list."

The day care dilemma is a painful struggle to find affordable care for your most precious possession by someone who will nurture your child precisely like you would. You won't find it. But you can find professional care in a clean, stimulating, nurturing environment. Do your homework. Get recommendations and visit the potential day care centers where you are considering placing your baby. Pay attention to smells. Is it clean? Do you smell old, dirty diapers?

Crying babies aren't an automatic negative. But pay attention to how long the same baby cries before someone comes to check the problem. Ask the teachers questions. Are they responsive to your inquiries? Do they want you to be involved with your child during the day? Will they report with gladness little steps in development your child takes? Are they accessible by phone? Some modern centers even have cameras positioned in your baby's room which enable you to check on your child through the Internet. You can pull up the center's Internet web site, click on your child's room, and observe him/her at play.

Is the center convenient to your workplace? You will be stressed enough without adding a double dose of traffic jousting every day.

Get a feel for the center. Intangibles, which only parental intuition can discern, make the difference between adequate and satisfying. Many discover that the day care expense of a second child makes it economically logical to stop working.

Priorities

A first child often doesn't noticeably slow down today's active families. A second child alters traffic patterns drastically! Trust me, I have two children and I speak from experience. But from the first, live your life so your growing child learns what's important. Don't let an infant keep you from attending worship services or attending to other religious, family, and community responsibilities.

A child is precious, immeasurably so. Too often, however, our culture revolves around children. Some social critics see evidence American culture is guilty of idolatry—and the false god is our children!

The Texas mother convicted of attempting to hire a contract killer to enhance her daughter's chances to make the high school cheerleading squad is an extreme, but is a factual example of parental desire to ensure a child's success. The idea was to murder the mother of another girl who was competing for the squad, causing enough emotional distress that she would fare poorly in the tryouts.

Perhaps fueled by guilt over investing so little time in our children, afraid they may reject us, haunted by the prospect of hurting their self-esteem by refusing any demand for the latest toy or not dressing them in the latest fashion fads, we open our checkbooks and wear out the magnetic strip on our credit cards.

In such an artificial environment, why shouldn't a child assume he/she anchors the universe? Every whim is granted and often anticipated. Parents explain away any loss or failure by blaming incompetent teachers, crooked referees, unfair conditions.

When a child is put at the center of everything, he gets a distorted view of the world, which revolved quite nicely before he arrived, thank you. Help your child, from the beginning, realize he is a part of a bigger world—a family—and that that family lives and loves and worships in a larger context. Love him, hug him, nurture him to eventually take his place in that bigger world.

It is helpful, and healthy, if she learns that other people, even—gasp!—her parents have rights and needs that sometimes outrank hers; that sometimes you don't win because the competition is better than you; and that, as all of us can attest, "Life isn't always fair."

Teach your children to function effectively in the real world, and the real world won't bewilder them.

Overlooked problems
- Five-year-olds not ready for school? Try Head Start.
- Pre-schoolers not healthy enough? How about Smart Start?
- Students having problems reading? Communities in Schools.
- Young people not investing in the country? AmeriCorps.
- Elderly need medical care? Medicare.
- People don't plan for their retirement years? Social Security.
- Big problems, big "solutions."

There's no room, time, or budget for individual solutions to small problems, like a single life adrift. If we have a problem with "teenagers in our community," city councils look for remedies they can prescribe for whole "groups."

What we really need are individual solutions because the problems are about individuals. What we really need is for individual adults to invest part of themselves in a single child adrift, and care for that child long enough to pull him to shore.

Every child needs a charismatic adult in his life, someone from whom to gather strength. Whether this person is a parent, relative, teacher, or coach; whether a child has one or two or even more in his life—these are not the important details. What matters is that at least one such person exists to give a child an edge.

Search your growing up memories. Who gave you the kind word or the encouraging smile at a critical time? Can you recall an emotional ache, a silent scream for someone—anyone in authority—to notice you and give you approval? Your children and all other children know exactly how you felt then. Try to remember yourself.

Such personal involvement by a charismatic, encouraging adult even helps insulate children from drug use and other delinquency.

How can one person make such a difference?

By giving a child the emotional permission to believe in himself or herself. Of course, faking it won't make it. Telling Susie she is the best soccer player on her team when she is a liability whenever the ball gets near her, or Johnny that his piano playing is divine when it crinkles the wallpaper, can have two outcomes—neither of them good. Either the child realizes that you are being untruthful and begins to discount everything you say, or believes you and develops the mother of all persecution complexes since no one else recognizes his or her marvelous talent.

Instead, pay close enough attention so that you can see where actual progress has been made and praise the effort the child put into making that advance. This teaches that obstacles are real but many can be overcome with work and patience.

Providing a "yes-I-can" attitude for a child is a big deal. It's what leads to resiliency. Kids' abilities to rebound from setbacks is a key to success in an increasingly complex world. And while all children need

79

resiliency, it is critical for those with low self-esteem, especially those who have learning or behavioral disabilities or whose home lives are unstable. What every child needs, and especially these kids, is to look in your eyes and see hope, not despair, encouragement rather than disappointment.

While a parent is the most obvious candidate to be the charismatic adult in a child's life, most of us can vouch that a teacher is often the adult who makes a difference. Teachers are perfectly positioned because they cannot only help a child believe in himself but can also provide situations where he can taste success.

Every child has something at which she can be successful. If her violin teacher despairs, how about art lessons? If team sports produce tears and bench time, explore individual athletic events. The successful teacher—and we all are teachers—matches ability with opportunity. A vast majority of those connections can and should happen at home. Celebrate reading a book, feeding the dog, washing the car, making cookies, committing random acts of kindness. Parents, teachers, neighbors, church school teachers, youth leaders, pastors, youth ministers, music ministers, uncles and aunts, bus stop buddies . . . the list of those who can be a significant, charismatic adult for a child is long. It just takes a willingness to quit hand-wringing and start talking.

Talk to the kid who rides his bike through your grass, or who walks by while you're in the yard, or who comes to your door to sell a magazine. Kneel down and greet the child in the corridor who seems all alone at church.

Call their names. That says you know them and to you, they are important. The solution for young people who can't seem to find direction in life is for someone like you to show them the way.

I had such a charismatic adult, my elementary and junior high school principal, Robert K. Hancock. He encouraged me to see beyond the cotton mills of Gastonia, N.C. He said I could soar when others would walk. He said I could sing when others would only mutter. And then he made me believe him.

I was a second grader, lugging the lunch plates from our classroom back to the kitchen when he made the first lasting contribution to who I would become. As I descended a long staircase, I fell, scattering dishes in all directions. I jumped up—and saw Mr. Hancock standing beside me. He didn't say a word. He brushed me off, made sure I was not hurt, helped me gather up the plates and sent me on my way. No embarrassing questions—just compassion, understanding, and concern.

He would drop into classrooms to teach, and to this day I consciously pattern my teaching style to his. He would call the entire student body together to listen to classical music. Classical music! In junior high school! Copies of great works of art decorated the entrance hall.

Mr. Hancock taught us that learning knows no boundaries and that most of our limitations are self-imposed. He pushed us to our intellectual limits and then gently took our hands and walked with us to the other side of our self-imposed boundaries. While others described the anchors that held me to earth, R.K. Hancock opened to me the wind and clouds that lifted me aloft.

Seek charismatic, energetic, encouraging teachers for your children; help your children's teachers be that way by encouraging them; and find a way to be that adult for your children, and someone else's.

Don't wait for a "big program" to fix the ills you see. Invest some of your life in another's. The big problem will begin to shrink—at the same time another life begins to loom large.

Strengthening the family unit

Many of the social changes in the latter part of the 20th century represent improvements, especially for women and minority adults. But the social consequences of family change over the past few decades have been largely negative, especially for children. Rather than criticize people who express concern over family decline, scholars and researchers would do better to address this question: Without strengthening the family unit, how can we possibly expect to improve the declining well-being of our children?

When a squalling newborn emerges into this world, the identity of its mother is never in question. But today it is not unusual for the father's identity to remain unknown, for any of many reasons, none of them good.

Initiatives like maternity homes, teen mother/baby homes, mother's aid, supplemented day care, and support groups help single moms cope with the hugely difficult task of raising their children alone.

It is hard enough to raise children with the help of a loving, compatible, tuned-in, caring and sharing spouse. To do it alone is a task of such magnitude it staggers me. But in our efforts to help mothers, perhaps we've made it too easy for men to become "fathers" without helping them be good "dads." At the same time, some fathers who want to be good dads are feeling shut out or helpless to know how to do it.

U.S. Census Bureau statistics show the number of single dads jumped 25 percent between 1995 and 1998. The trend is most prevalent in America's cities where women addicted to drugs and alcohol abandon their families.

North Carolina numbers are even more startling. The percentage of dads with sole custody of their children jumped 66 percent between 1995 and 1997— to six percent of all households in the state.

These facts challenge the myth that men have little more to contribute to child rearing than a paycheck. Single men are proving to courts and adoption agencies that they are sound caretakers.

A few initiatives around the country are beginning to focus on the issue of "fathering," including one at Baptist Children's Homes designed to address the problem in Davidson County, where our oldest campus and system administration offices are located.

Three focus groups were held. They included groups for fathers of children in day care and those who were interested in the spiritual dimension of fatherhood. A third group was held at Davidson County Community College for young men who are fathers but are not married to the mothers of their children.

The confidential discussions welcomed all responses to such questions as:

- what do you like most about being a father?
- how might children be disadvantaged by the lack of good fathering?
- how do fathers learn to be good fathers?
- are there barriers fathers have to deal with in being "good fathers"?
- what can the community do to help men be better fathers?
- if only one thing could be accomplished initially, what would you like for that to be?

What an interesting idea—asking fathers how they evaluate the situation instead of simply mandating solutions!

This initiative has grown to be the focus of All Children Together (ACT), a countywide coalition of caring services assembled with the help of both a planning and operating grant from The Duke Endowment in Charlotte, N.C. ACT members have formed their own board and will forge initiatives to make fathering a bellwether issue in Davidson County. It is hoped this will provide a model that other states and counties will follow.

Here are a few reasons why it's important:

● Nearly one-quarter of U.S. children now live in a home without a father (biological, adoptive, or stepfather).

● About 1.2 million of the nation's children will be born out of wedlock this year, about one-third of all births.

● Every year more than a million new children suffer from the divorce of their parents.

● Although teenagers spend an average of 21 hours watching TV each week, they spend an average 35 minutes per week talking to their fathers, according to a study released as the 20th century concluded.

Suddenly, it has become fashionable to talk about fatherhood. "For too many years we've been engaged in collective amnesia about the importance of fathers in the lives of children," said Ronald Mincy of the Ford Foundation, which has underwritten a national "Fragile Families" program to support and study fatherhood in poor communities. Leaders in the movement blame the prevalence of divorce and out-of-wedlock births for minimizing the father's role in child rearing. The result: more children are living in poverty and children are more likely to drop out of school, get involved in drugs or crime, and treat their own children poorly.

At the heart of the movement to help men be better fathers are efforts to reinvigorate fatherhood in the inner city, where the consequences of fatherless families are most dire. According to the National Center for Health Statistics, 66 percent of black children are not living with their biological father, more than twice the percentage for white children.

Although Davidson County, N.C., has no large cities, the model we've established here could be emulated throughout the state, and elsewhere.

We are for families. Where we can help fathers be better fathers, and help mothers be better mothers, we help preserve families and make life better for everyone in them.

Doing activities together

An old hymn assures us "Blest be the Tie that Binds." The slogan "The family that prays together, stays together" has a first cousin: "The family that plays together stays together." The Bible says our treasure, the things we value most, resides where our hearts live, where we invest our emotional energy.

Ergo, if we treasure our children our hearts will tune in to them. And as we invest our hearts in them our children become ever greater treasures.

Ties that bind loving parents to their children, and vice versa, keep the children healthier and safer. Researchers found that parents have a greater influence in the lives of their children than they could imagine, or their children generally admit. Though teenagers may love freedom and snap against restraints, the research says that older children with close ties to their parents are less likely to consider suicide, have sex at an early age, smoke, drink, take drugs, or become violent.

Those findings were among the first results from a massive survey of American youth, designed by two University of North Carolina at Chapel Hill sociologists, that call into question a lot of the conventional wisdom about teen culture.

One of those beliefs is that other teenagers, rather than parents, hold the greatest sway over how teens behave. Much of American culture has bought into the idea that once our children hit puberty the only thing that matters to them is their peer group. Mom's and Dad's opinions may be, at best, kindly tolerated but they don't enter into the equation.

Another part of the survey notes: "Teenagers are very skillful at convincing us that we have become irrelevant in their lives. But parents' expectations, values, and connectedness are fundamentally important." That statement alone provides enough ammunition for parents to stay in the battle for its duration. No one has to wave the white flag when children hit the teenage years. They still watch everything you do.

Your teens will stretch and kick against the boundaries, but they want to know where the boundaries are. And they want to know you are patrolling the borders.

I've seen teens shake their heads in amazement and heard them talk about friends who have no curfews—and nobody home to care if they are out all night.

These teens aren't wishing for the same "freedoms." They're glad for guidelines and for somebody at home who cares.

In fact, I am convinced that teens value the approval of adults—but only from adults they respect and admire, adults whose lives exhibit integrity and consistency and who know the teens as individuals.

One simple step to earning that status is to learn names. Get to know and use the names of the little children with whom you come into contact. Anonymity breeds poor behavior. They don't think you know who they are, so what can you do?

When I call our residents and staff by name, I see their shoulders straighten and their countenances brighten. Everyone wants to leave a mark in the world. Children want to know they are known. The sweetest sound to any of us is still the sound of our own name.

Diffusing dangerous actions

We all mourn the tragic waste of lives and potential to drug use, the "children killing children" epidemic, the logic-defying behavior of mixing fast cars and alcohol as a teen rite of passage.

So what do we do about it?

Perhaps the National Longitudinal Study of Adolescent Health, the largest attempt ever to better understand what conditions increase risky behavior among youth, can give us some clues.

Over a three-year period, researchers surveyed 90,000 children in grades seven to 12 in their schools and then questioned 12,105 children in their homes. Using 500 surveyors, they questioned parents and teachers to get a fuller sense of each child's environment.

They found:

● The presence of drugs, alcohol, or tobacco at home increases the chance that the children will use them.

● Adolescents who live with guns are more likely to engage in violence or attempt suicide.

● Children who consider religion and prayer important tend to wait longer to have sex; are less likely to drink, smoke, or use drugs.

Michael C. Blackwell

While it emphasizes risky behavior, the study also provides encouragement to parents since the findings include the upbeat assertion that while "too many kids smoke, too many engage in sex at a young age, and too many experiment with drugs, most adolescents are good kids. Most are doing fine."

Unfortunately "most" isn't nearly enough. Another academic study, this one of 12,105 teenagers, found:

- 25.1 percent have been victims of crimes
- 17.5 percent drank alcohol at least once a month
- 12.5 percent had carried a weapon in the past month
- 6.9 percent have considered suicide

Mastering the money monster

If your mailbox is at all like mine, it attracts a constant stream of free money offers from credit card and home equity loan companies that want to take the wait out of your life. You can have everything you want right now and pay for it on an easy schedule. If you're not careful, you can easily dig a personal debt hole big enough to bury you.

People who didn't learn the value of money and the work required to obtain it as children don't do well managing their funds as adults. We may not like discussing money with our children, but we should do so. According to estimates by Children's Market Research, America's kids spend $7 billion a year on candy, gum, snacks, and video games when they're young, and on clothing, video games, cosmetics, and CDs when they are older.

Where do they get that money? From allowances, chores, baby-sitting, jobs, and gifts. Yet some kids with an allowance never have money, and some kids with no allowance always have a dollar in their pocket because they do odd jobs and have been taught how to manage their money.

Responsible parents teach children how to save and how to spend wisely. An allowance helps children learn to manage money and is one of the best ways to teach financial responsibility.

How large should an allowance be? This question isn't as complicated as computing your income tax, but still has enough variables to eschew easy answers. The simple extremes of giving them whatever they want whenever they ask or not giving them anything should be avoided, but family income, children's ages, even the child's "cost-of-living" should be considered.

Allowance provides an opportunity to educate your sons and daughters about many areas that will be vital in their adult lives. Of course, wise money management is one but things like delayed gratification, generosity, realistic goal setting, and pooling resources for common good are also important. In other words, "You can't always get what you want but sometimes you get what you need."

Total what you and/or your child currently spend on lunches, movies, and clothing. Add what you feel the child should save or donate to charity—that is a starting point. However, the amount the child gives to the church and charity has great potential to turn into a swamp.

You should teach and encourage the practice and you can suggest an amount or percentage (while being sure you practice what you preach). But if you force the issue, the child is apt to learn nothing except that churches and charities drain her/his money through pressure and guilt. Better to let them experience the true joy of giving from a free will.

You may not be ready to give the child responsibility for all those items. Obviously a six-year-old (and a lot of 16-year-olds) lack the maturity to manage. A few failures and the lessons learned might be appropriate for the teenager.

As a fiscally responsible parent teaching fiscal responsibility to your children, the main thing is to have a clear and mutual understanding of what the allowance covers. Don't include movie money in the allowance, then be susceptible to a plea for extra money to see the latest *Star Wars* prequel. This helps the child grasp the fact that gifts in addition to the allowance are truly gifts, that it is not a parental obligation to supply every whim of fashion and fad.

Under this system children become responsible for spending decisions. If they spend a month's allowance on a pair of jeans, they have to live with the consequences of no other new clothes that month. Requests for big-ticket items such as games, bicycles, clothing, and sports equipment can be used to teach about goal setting. Help your children set up schedules of extra chores to earn the money, decide how many weeks it will take and develop a plan to achieve that goal.

Older children need to learn about the dangers of credit. A credit card purchase is really a loan, which we promise to pay back with interest—and the interest is quite high. Some parents charge their children interest on small loans to teach them how expensive it is to "rent someone else's money."

A young friend of mine, who shall remain nameless to protect the guilty, received an unsolicited check in the mail for $3,600. All he had to do was deposit the check and start spending the money. What he failed to notice was it was no ordinary check. It was a loan that charged nearly 20 percent interest!

His mother—who also shall remain nameless—had to pick up the payments for this "oversight." I understand that the father, a calm and reasonable man, took his son's prized Michael Jordan rookie basketball card as collateral and will keep it until the loan is repaid.

Others tell me of college students accepting the "free" credit cards which bombard their mail boxes, running up thousands and thousands of dollars of high-interest debt before they finally have to confess to their parents. Some even have to drop out of college, unable to feed the plastic maw and pay tuition at the same time.

Discuss advertising. Point out that advertisements are created to make a product appear attractive and exciting. Teach your youngster about the dangers of impulse buying. When you go shopping, use a list. Discuss how easy it is to spend extra money when you purchase something that "catches your eye" rather than something you need or want.

Children are never too young to learn to save, and to be generous to church and others. Teaching financial responsibility early will enable your children to be financially independent as adults, and to avoid the source of many of the arguments that stress marriages to the breaking point—money.

Gambling—seductive road to self-destruction

With sweepstakes entry forms arriving in the mail almost daily, a fresh wave of "big money windfall" hysteria washes through the land. Most of us daydream, at least occasionally, about being rich. And we love the idea of lots of "free money" falling into our laps without effort.

Knowing a desire for riches infects so many, the hardest job for the gambling industry is simply to get state legislatures to allow them to pick citizens' pockets. Once approved, the industry builds the mousetraps, and the mice troop in to throw their funds toward their own witless slaughter.

The gambling industry (which prefers to call itself "gaming industry") thrives because it has convinced even citizens who disapprove of the activity that it is harmless, voluntary; that it raises revenue for socially acceptable and necessary causes without the pain of taxation.

But men like Ed Looney know the real horror story of gambling pain. Looney is executive director of the New Jersey Council on Compulsive Gambling, which runs a national hotline for gamblers in trouble. Looney tells of one 16-year-old who slit his wrists after losing $6,000, four years of newspaper delivery earnings, on the lottery in a single day. A college student dropped out of school because he lost his tuition money gambling. One 19-year-old youth sold his car for a fraction of its value so he could get back into the casinos. Numerous kids are too scared to go back to school because they can't pay their bookies.

Thousands of young people fall victim to America's gambling obsession every year. Authorities say more than a million adolescents are already addicted to gambling.

The most addictive forms of gambling, eagerly promoted by more and more state governments in search of tax revenues, are undermining families, hurting communities, and destroying civic order.

An estimated 10 million Americans have an out-of-control gambling habit. When gambling activities are legalized and made accessible in new jurisdictions, the number of addicted gamblers increases anywhere from 100 to 550 percent. The casino industry is heavily dependent on the revenues of psychologically sick people. Economists calculate that more than half of a casino's take comes from problem and pathological gamblers.

Studies show that children of compulsive gamblers are almost twice as likely to experience the trauma of a broken home. In Harrison County, MS, the hub of the state's casino industry, the number of divorces rose from 440 in 1992 to nearly 1,100 in 1993, the first full year after casinos were legalized.

It's very odd that so many states are now legalizing and promoting activities that were absolutely illegal not that long ago. What is a lottery but a "numbers racket" that police and FBI agents have been engaged in fighting for years?

Legalized gambling of the new kind increases crime of the old kind. Three years after casinos came in, Atlantic City rose from 50th to first in the nation among cities in per capita crime. Within five years of permitting limited-stakes casinos in Deadwood, SD, serious crimes jumped 93 percent. A year after welcoming casinos in 1992, bank robberies along Mississippi's Gulf Coast had increased from one to 13, and armed robberies tripled. In the three years after Foxwoods, the nation's richest casino, opened in Ledyard, CT, rape, robbery, car theft, and larceny all increased more than 400 percent.

Maryland government official J. Joseph Curran, Jr., issued a report concluding that: "Casinos would bring a substantial increase in crime to our state. There would be more violent crime, more crimes against property, more insurance fraud, more white-collar crime, more juvenile crime, more drug and alcohol-related crime, more domestic violence and child abuse, and more organized crime."

Thank goodness some state governing bodies are still keeping an eye on the gambling industry so that our most innocent citizens will be protected.

Chapter Nine

Inside strength training:
nurturing and nursing
your child's inner child

Children today are tyrants.
They contradict their parents, gobble their food,
and tyrannize their teachers.
                                        —Socrates

You don't have to suffer
to be a poet;
adolescence is enough suffering
for anyone.
        —John Ciardi

I went to the garden
To pick a rose for the one I love.
I found a pink one, the last.
I smiled as I cut it.
But as I put it into the vase,
The petals fell off.
The petals fell off.
The petals fell off.
The story of my life.
The petals fell off,
And I was left with
A stem and thorns,
As usual.

                                        —Shante, BCH child

Every time I encounter a strong, courageous, vibrant human being,
I remind myself that that person did not come by those attributes all by
himself or herself. Back of every personality lies one of the oldest and
most significant of all human arts—the art of parenting.

It is a process that includes much more than a biological act of conception and birth. That's the easy part. The process goes on for years and at different stages calls for all kinds of skill and ingenuity. To take a newborn infant who at the moment of birth is nothing but a bundle of needs and potentialities and carefully nurture and guide that crying infant until a fully functioning human being emerges—that is as great an art as there is. When it is done well, all of us profit and the quality of human life is improved. When it is done poorly, not only the child, but all of us suffer in terms of crime and misery that result.

I am not sure who has the right to speak about the art of parenting because all of us who wear the label of parent have blown it many times. The reason I risk doing so is because I firmly believe that parents can make a difference in a child's life.

Several years ago I came across—and kept—an article called "Ten Commandments of Successful Parenting." I have made my own modifications to the Rev. Dr. L.D. Johnson's words, and would call them "Commandments For New Millennium Families—10 ways you can soar above the coming flood of change."

1. Thou shalt enforce rules with flexibility

    No child should grow up without rules. Everyone needs a structure for life. Rules indicate that parents care. Permissive child rearing is a tragic notion. At the same time, the rules should be tempered by common sense and should provide structure with flexibility while being consistent. Don't send mixed signals to your children.

2. Thou shalt love unconditionally

    A child's security comes from the knowledge of his parents' unconditional love. If he or she has that, the child can endure almost any other deprivation without being emotionally crippled. Genuine love does not say "I will love you if" or "I love you because." It simply says, "I love you. You are my child. In spite of all you have done or may do, I will always love you."

    As old as my children are, they always blossom when I show appreciation, affirmation, love, and support. In fact, they crave it and I love to give it to them.

3. Thou shalt discipline appropriately

The clue to healthy discipline is to remember that the basic meaning of that word is "teaching." It is not to vent our own anger, or to inflict punishment, or to show who is boss. Sometimes we say to our children, "I hope that teaches you a lesson." With the proper tone of voice, that is the reason to discipline—to teach a lesson. Be sure the punishment fits the crime. Discipline appropriately.

4. Thou shalt explain fully

The human mind, especially at an early age, is a thirsty sponge eager to soak up limitless amounts of information and experience. Greatest mistake—never showing a child that you love her or him. Second greatest mistake—never taking the time to explain. Our beliefs, our hopes, our views of life, faith, and the real world should be communicated to our children. Explain them fully.

5. Thou shalt praise generously

Most of us are quicker with complaint than with gratitude. It is easier to fire off criticism than commendation. There is tremendous power in sincere praise. We would all be better persons and have stronger families if we were more generous with praise. Mark Twain said, "I can live for two months on a good compliment." We should not have to wait that long. Do not withhold approval and affirmation. Praise generously. Your child wants your approval. Give it whenever you can.

6. Thou shalt show affection warmly

Remember the bumper sticker that asked, "Have you hugged your child today?" The child with parents who are affectionate towards him feels good about himself. The child who is not shown love and does not see love may become a cold, affectionless adult. Show affection warmly. Your child needs it, yearns for it, thrives on it, and grows because of it.

7. Thou shalt listen closely

Are you a listener, a lecturer, a griper, a nagger, a complainer to your children? Are your ideas and your ailments the most important items on your agenda? Or do you really listen to others, especially do you listen to your children? They have interesting ideas and express themselves uniquely. Listen up!

8. When thou art wrong, thou shalt admit it readily

    One of the toughest sentences we ever utter is, "I'm sorry, I was wrong." As parents we have a terrible time saying it to our children. Why are we so threatened by admitting that we made a mistake? We are not infallible. No one is right all the time. It's healthy and therapeutic to admit our mistakes.

9. Thou shalt choose thy environment thoughtfully

    If you want your children to be good people, associate with good people. If you care whether they love and serve God, you will involve your family in a community of faith. Choose your environment thoughtfully, carefully, and prayerfully. It can make all the difference in the life of your child.

10. Thou shalt model carefully

    Values are more caught than taught. We model our values for our children. If parents are compassionate, caring, and thoughtful, chances are their children will be too. If, on the other hand, parents are profane, careless about what is sacred, and are selfish in their attitudes, so also will be their children. Model carefully because your children will mirror you.

The Bible lifts the idea of parenthood to an even greater dimension. Jesus called God "Father." He described God in human terms because that is the only way people would understand. He described God in parenting terms. God is the ultimate in strength and provision, qualities we can associate with father/mother. God is the ultimate in love and compassion which we can associate with mother/father. In our own parenting we are modeling the love of God for our children.

Jesus implied that a human parent is a model of our Heavenly Parent. This leads to a tough question for anyone who is a parent: What kind of God do you portray?

How do we transmit our values?

One of the deepest desires of a parent is to bequeath a legacy of heartfelt values to his or her child. To pass along convictions and principles that have become a part of us through our experience is not only our responsibility but demonstrates deep love for our offspring.

Taking a few common sense steps will go a long way toward imparting an understanding of what values are important to you, why they are important, and why you want your child to embrace those values.

1. Treat your child with respect in every situation, especially when sharing significant beliefs.

    Much of what you wish to convey to your child will be accepted or rejected based merely on its presentation. If you treat your child fairly and with dignity, you're creating an open environment in which the child will feel free to listen and speak. If a child feels you're talking down to him, he may block the message. Sometimes adults forget children need to feel respected and that their fragile feelings need protecting. Children deserve value, worth, and dignity.

2. Listen to your child.

    Truly hear what your child is saying or asking as related to the values you are sharing. Many times, we as adults assume our words are crystal clear to children and the way we say things has the same meaning to our children as it does to us.

    If you listen with all your senses, you can determine if your child is both hearing and understanding you. To be a good listener, you should listen for feelings and seek to empathize. Concentrate on your child. Look into his eyes and enter into his thoughts and experiences.

    Avoid "pat" answers. Your first response may be easiest, but bite your tongue and think more deeply about the question. Your child will know if you are simply repeating platitudes to her without concern for really hearing her.

    Children who ask "Why?" aren't just trying to drive us crazy. They really want to know what makes things work and why we hold the values we do and why it is important that they hold them, too. It takes time and effort to truly listen, but the results are well worth the effort.

3. Be aware that you are an example.

    There is no question that you are an example: the question is what kind of example are you? If your actions are not consistent with your words, there is slim chance your "lecture" will mean anything to its audience. Your life—conduct, speech, choices, and actions—forms the basis for your witness to your child. The old saying is true: "If a child lives with criticism, he will criticize."

What your child observes in you is what he internalizes, far sooner and more permanently than anything you say to him. Make sure your life speaks the values you want to impart. Be an authentic model for your child to emulate. Your values will begin to be reflected in the actions of your child. (See commandment 10.)

4. Encourage and affirm.

When your child makes progress in behavior and demonstrates your values, praise lavishly but sincerely. Encouragement helps your child embrace your values and gives vital messages about esteem, confidence, and courage. The way children feel about themselves is determined in great measure by their perception of how you feel about them. Success begets success. Encouraging and supporting your children does wonders in moving them along toward an acceptance of those values which will have great meaning in their lives.

5. Love your child unconditionally and make sure he/she knows it.

This is the most important ingredient in building a lasting relationship of trust and acceptance. Children are remarkably intuitive: they can sense and feel if you're authentic. They know if things aren't the way you say they are. Mistakes will be made but love forgives all. You won't always like your child's actions but you can always love your child. Children may not always remember the gifts you give them but they will never forget the fact that you loved them. (See commandment 2.)

- Respect your child
- Listen to your child
- Be an example for your child
- Love your child
- Encourage and affirm your child

If you follow these common sense guidelines, you'll achieve far more than the splendid accomplishment of building a strong, loving, and enduring relationship with your child or children. You'll build a foundation for your values that will outlive you in the lives of your descendants. Such will be your legacy.

Transmitting values to your child requires a continuing, shared experience. To have a lasting impact, values must be learned over an extended time. The result is a lifetime relationship between loving parent and loving child.

More simple ways to instill values

What characterizes the home learning environment in which children are most likely to succeed? According to the National Committee for Citizens in Education, children fare best:

- When parents establish regular bedtimes and a daily family routine
- When parents monitor television viewing and other out-of-school activities
- When parents express high but realistic expectations for achievement
- When parents stimulate reading, writing, and discussions among family members
- When parents help with homework and provide access to newspapers, encyclopedias and other home learning tools
- When parents encourage use of libraries, museums, and other community resources. (I would add: Parents also need to closely monitor their child's usage of the Internet, which is rapidly replacing traditional sources of information.)

Just as family interactions around the dinner table pay surprising dividends, the number and variety of learning tools (books, tapes, puzzles, sets of encyclopedia, computers and the like) in the home have a profound effect on student achievement.

Educators agree that the number of learning tools available in the home is a much stronger predictor of academic achievement than factors such as whether parents expect children to attend college. Your home environment is definitely an influence on your child's development. Make it a positive one.

Inspire, encourage your children

Do any of the cases feel familiar?

- Sharon, a former star student, never does her homework anymore. Instead she spends all her class time giggling with friends.
- An eleven-year-old comes home depressed, a wrinkled paper in his hand. It's not a demerit or rejection, it's his first grade that is not

an "A."

● Lisa is a hardworking girl who makes a positive difference in her classroom and impresses her teachers. But she doesn't feel she will ever live up to her parents' expectations.

What can parents do to help children achieve at their highest level? How can concerned parents walk the fine line between encouragement and expectation, and being overdemanding and stress inducing?

Begin by teaching yourself to show an encouraging interest while keeping the child's identity and yours separate. That can be tough when our egos see an opportunity to make up for some of our own insecurities by reversing the "my dad can beat your dad" scenario to one that plays out in the classroom (my kid is smarter than your kid), the athletic field (my kid scored four goals today—how'd your klutz of a daughter do?), or lifestyle (my kid is going to Italy to study art this summer, too bad your kid doesn't have the talent—and you don't have the money).

A good friend from Texas, a sports writer, sent me a column he wrote about a football game in a small South Texas town near Corpus Christi. In Texas, football short-circuits the logic function in the brains of most of the population. (Which goes to show what they know. The only legitimate medical cause for such an effect is Atlantic Coast Conference basketball.)

In a play-off game, the home team's star halfback shattered his leg. As he pulled himself toward the sideline with his arms, his father's voice boomed out: "Get back in there son, we need you." It doesn't take a rocket scientist to deduce the father valued the secondary glory *he* got from his son the halfback more than he valued his son as his son.

You are not living through your child, trying to make up for your own failures or to reproduce "perfection" for you in your child. He or she is a separate person. Your goal is to help your child become everything God intends him or her to be. Your goal should not be to clone another adult who is just like you or who succeeds where you failed.

Such an approach requires that you know your son or daughter as an individual. So get out of your chair, turn off the television and your computer, put down the paper, stay home tonight, unplug the phone, and talk with your child.

Share you own interests. Musicians tend to have musical children, scientists have children interested in science, English teachers give birth to children who read at the breakfast table and under the covers at night—and it isn't all genetic. If parents are accessible and communication flows easily both ways, the things that deeply interest them will be of interest to their children—at least enough to explore a bit.

Be aware of chances to encourage and expand some interest the child may express. If your child wonders how whales live in the ocean without gills, take him to the library for books on the ocean, or sit down at the computer and check various Internet sites. (Information—and misinformation—can readily be found about almost any subject on the Internet.)

Finally, being a lifelong learner yourself is perhaps the best advice I can give parents who are interested in their child's drive for excellence. *School is never out for the savvy parent.* Encourage your child to be an intellectual explorer, to go beyond the minimum requirements, to chase after information about things that interest them.

Winners of the Westinghouse Science Contest say they drew their inspiration from many different life experiences, not only academic pursuits. A parent is the best person to provide such experiences.

- Take your child to concerts, plays and lectures, poetry readings, museums and science fairs.
- Play "what if" games.
- Support your child's interests even if they're not your own. Even if this is hard, or seemingly impossible, give it your best try.
- Get your child a library card.
- Keep books, magazines, and newspapers around the house.
- Read the newspaper together.
- Take turns reading favorite books aloud.
- Help your child develop good homework skills.
- Be sure your five-year-old has his orange to take to school to make fruit salad.
- If your 10-year-old is doing a report on wolves, help her find the information she needs.
- Teach your child the direct relationship between hard work and achievement. Thomas Edison once said, "Genius is one percent

inspiration and 99 percent perspiration."

● Let her see what goes into baking a birthday cake, growing the perfect tomato, or fixing the engine of a car.

● Read biographies of famous people and discuss them.

● At the start of each semester/quarter/learning unit help her make a list of things she wants to accomplish. Refer to the list periodically and talk about the progress she is making.

● Don't undermine her teacher with criticism.

● Don't take him out of school early and bring him back late to stretch out your vacation.

● Help your child to think about long-term goals, such as college and future careers.

● At moments of discouragement, tell your child about a time you failed; that you faced and feared important tests too or didn't get elected to the student council or got cut from the baseball team. Explain how you overcame the failure and used it as a springboard to move on to new things.

Help kids grow through failure

One of the most important—but most painful—lessons everyone has to learn is that we can't always be perfect, that we can't always control the situation or wish away unpleasant consequences.

Failing (also read: rejection) is painful for anyone, no matter how old. That's why it's a double whammy for parents when our children fail: we feel their hurt as much as we do our own, and we want to make it better. Yet, as instinctive as it is to want to take the hurt away, it can be the wrong thing to do, especially if it's all we do.

Failing is something everyone experiences throughout life. The earlier kids learn to cope with it, the better they'll be. Just as we should seek legitimate venues where our children can experience success, we need to stand back many times when they look as if they are going to fail, as long as they don't risk permanent damage. As hard as it is, it's a developmental task we need to allow. Failing does not equate with being a failure. Failing is a necessary building block for character.

The first line for parents to draw is between what you consider "failing" and what your child does. What's insignificant to you may be a big deal to him. I once heard a Tennessee preacher explain a similar point: "When your teenager's heart is broken by what you know is 'puppy love,' remember that the pain is real to the puppy."

For a child, a feeling of failing generally comes from something in which she invests a lot of effort and ego, but which doesn't work out. A five-year-old who spends days repeatedly trying to ride a two-wheeler may feel like a failure, but a child who tries it once in a while probably won't.

While it's critical to offer sympathy, there's another fine line to draw: between feeling sorry for her and validating her hurt.

Focus on the future, even with a two-year-old. The sun will come up tomorrow even if we spend all night swimming in a pity pool. It's never too young to start learning (and never too old to forget) the **FIDO** strategy: **F**orget **I**t, **D**rive **O**n! If a toddler spills a glass of milk, give her some paper towels to clean it up. The message she gets is not only that a mistake isn't the end of the world, but also that she has the power to fix it. Later, talk about what she can do so she might not spill next time: Was the glass too close to the edge, too full, too tipsy?

With toddlers and preschoolers, child psychologists suggest separating the failure from the child and, especially with four and five-year-olds, offering praise for effort: "You did your best didn't you—then it's okay. You look at the things you did improve on—way to go!"

Preschoolers are especially vulnerable to defeat by failures—practically every waking action is a challenge—and therefore sometimes they will not want to try again. They also may equate failure with being a bad person.

But if parents can help their preschoolers learn to relish a challenge, they will come to understand that never giving up is the standard bedrock of the road to success. This inoculates their self-esteem so that an episode of failing is tied to a single event or effort and carries no permanent damage.

With school, children begin massive encounters with RULES. It is a particularly vulnerable time for "mistakes" because there are so many things you can do wrong—forget to raise your hand; kick the soccer ball with your toe instead of the side of your foot; put your hand over the wrong side of your chest during the pledge of allegiance; somehow do something to get "cooties."

Because of the intensity children feel about the rules and regulations for schoolwork and social behavior and sports, anything other than the prescribed order feels like failure in a pass-fail system.

By age nine or so and continuing through the teenage years, kids tend to generalize from a failure. This is potentially the most destructive scenario. A seventh grader who fails a math test might think, "I'm stupid, I can't do anything right." Suddenly, she's having problems with her friends, with athletics, in other subjects. Her generalization becomes a self-fulfilling prophecy.

The antidote is to help your child keep a failure in perspective, and to offer ideas on how to prevent it from happening again. When he asserts he is stupid because he failed a spelling test, help him study for the next test. If she's feeling worthless, see if her older sister or a favorite relative can include her in an activity so she feels grown up.

With any age child, it's also helpful to understand a child's logic. Be sure it isn't faulty assumptions or bad information giving him an internal reading of "failure." If you know how he thinks, you are better positioned to help him succeed next time.

The way to do this is to ask questions rather than pass judgment. The one question to avoid is, "Why did you do that?" Even if you don't add the words, "you stupid kid you," your child still hears them and he feels defensive, defeated, and stupid. Soon, he'll stop trying altogether.

Instead ask non-judgmental questions: "Can we check out those instructions together? . . . Were you thinking about missing your friend who moved away when you were working on this? . . . What were you hoping to wind up with when you started?"

Finally, don't forget you can tell a child he or she is special and a success in your eyes and heart without using words. You literally can touch them where they hurt.

One great thing, among many, of working where I do is that I have a job I can hug. When I'm feeling low, or overwhelmed, I can visit a room full of kids and be rejuvenated with a hug. Remember the bumper stickers that said, "Have you hugged your child today?" They're nice reminders and I support the sentiment.

Authentic, loving hugs are medicine for a weary heart and glue for emotional bonding that you can get virtually no other way.

We are not a very touchy society, despite our seeming preoccupation with sensuality. Other societies are "close talkers" and hand holders. People drape arms around friend's shoulders when talking intensely.

But Americans tend to interpret all touching as sexual, so we avoid it lest our action be misinterpreted. We miss out on a lot. Are you hugging enough as you struggle to raise loving children who know they are loved? Do you send your children to school with an abundance of hugs and keep them from getting the insecurity germ?

Do your children see you hugging your spouse so they know you are "together" and they are secure? I'm told a child needs 10-20 real hugs and kisses every day. Are you a few shy from the supply side? We can truly touch our families when we realize the power of touch God has put into our hands.

Chapter Ten

All about doing time:
you can pay it now
or they can pay later

> *Americans have begun to understand*
> *that trouble does not start somewhere*
> *on the other side of town.*
> *It seems to originate inside the absolute*
> *middle of the homemade cherry pie.*
> *—June Jordan*

> *Some mothers and fathers can trace their ancestors back*
> *three hundred years, but they can't tell you where*
> *their children were last night.*
> *—Anonymous*

> *All around me I see darkness-*
> *Not just dim shadows, but pure black.*
> *Everything feels rough and dreary.*
> *I wish I were home.*
> *But wait . . .*
> *Home is where I just ran away from.*
> *—Dawn, BCH child*

Riding roller coasters with your legs dangling free at 80 miles an hour? Yawn. Big-as-a-house screens with movies so realistic you're splashed by waves and get seasick when the whales dive? Yeah, right.

Video games with enough blood and mayhem that some parents ban them from the house? Good move; such things should be banned from any house where children live. The lifestyle of New Millennium Families will amass experiences faster than Jeff Gordon circles a racetrack. Do this, taste that, see this, go there, buy that, hear this, try that. When a child's senses stay stimulated to the max, life can become a series of yawns. No pace seems too fast, no image too vivid or violent, no experience too exciting.

Therapists, teachers, and parents are calling for time out. Experts are concerned about whether this ongoing sensory salvo—and the subsequent lack of down time—has consequences that no one has thoroughly studied or yet understands. Our children are being swept up into a faster and faster pace.

Their parents grew up with television, fast cars, and loud music, too. But the level of intensity, the speed of delivery, and the constant bombardment by many forms of media have reached a peak. And, when these children watch their own parents tear through life at breakneck speed, the message becomes "the fast life equals the good life."

Children are overstimulated. So many don't know how to entertain themselves, or deal with a quiet moment. They feel an hour without the television or radio blaring away is punishment. What if Isaac Newton, reclining with his back against an apple tree one warm summer day, had been plugged in to a portable CD player when the apple fell beside him? He probably would never have noticed and we still wouldn't understand gravity!

In BCH's day care centers, we remind parents not to allow their children to bring certain toys or wear clothing picturing violent cartoon characters. Warrior toys prompt aggressive behavior. Children need to be removed from such overstimulating situations so they can calm down. While you might be able to endure the results with your own two or three children, put them in a classroom with 15 other children and duck.

As adults, we know the value of quiet time, which accounts for the boom in sales of CDs and tapes of relaxation music. Despite that knowledge, we often don't have the common sense to put it into practice. Obviously, children need to be taught the importance of being still, mentally, emotionally, and physically.

Have you ever watched an adult take her first roller coaster ride? Or can you remember your own, the face stretching velocity, the Hundred Years War in your stomach? Watch the youngest children today. Most likely they will exhibit no fear nor scream (involuntarily). They've been there and done that. (I vividly recall my first—and last— roller coaster ride: summer of 1969. Myrtle Beach, S.C. I promised the Lord that if he let me survive, I would become a vegetarian and call my mother every Sunday.)

It is the children suffering from the extremes of constant over-stimulation and lack of quiet time who often end up in doctors' offices with such symptoms as insomnia, anxiety, irritability, and hyperactivity or emergency rooms with life systems battered by car wrecks, extreme sports, drug overdoses, or gang wounds. Or maybe they land in juvenile court or, worst yet, they wind up dead.

The speed of life for many children today is so fast, that only by moving faster and faster can they stay alert and interested. It is a problem manifesting itself in classrooms, churches, movie theaters, and even at the family dinner table (or family TV trays) when members eat standing up, looking at their watches.

Are your children so wound up they don't want to go to bed at night? Are you feeding into the go-go cycle that prompts your child to become bored at the first sign of slowing down? Some people argue that there are no good computer, television, or video games when it comes to small children since such "addiction to stimulation" teaches our children to have zero attention spans.

My eyeballs vibrate to watch some of the current television commercials, aimed at a younger set. Images flash across the screen for fractions of a second. Such brief flashes are probably effective because they demand that the viewer pay attention to catch the message. Young eyes are bored with an image that stays on screen a whole second or two.

Face it. We are modeling life for the next generation. If we demand that life move faster so we can "do" more, working into the night to "have" more, it is no surprise our children demand a faster pace so they can "feel" more. Help them realize "time out" is not a punishment of silence, but a temporary slowing down that will enable them to hear new music.

Hard choices prevent hard time

Not only will a slower pace demand less stimulation, it also will provide more opportunities and options for parents and children to keep up with each other.

In families where that doesn't happen, the first call always seems to be unexpected. You're at home or in the office and a police officer or store manager tells you over the phone that your child is being held for stealing, or destruction of property, or fighting, or dealing drugs.

Maybe you've been so out of touch you don't notice your child's behavior slipping toward delinquent, even criminal behavior. Maybe you have seen the signs, but struggled fiercely and didn't know what to do about them.

Law enforcement officials and psychologists have put together guidelines on how to react when your child gets into trouble. Although dealing with the legal system is a serious matter, the parents' task of getting the child back on the right track is equally important.

Here are some guidelines if your child must deal with the legal system:

1. Brainstorm about the possible reasons the child might have committed his infraction or is in a position to be suspected of it. It is important to try to know "why" to determine the best course of action.

2. Parents should ask themselves these kinds of questions:
- Is the child or family going through a particularly stressful time and is this a cry for help?
- Has the child learned that he is more likely to get attention for acting inappropriately than when he behaves?
- Then again, could materialism be the root cause?

3. Get involved with the child's life. Parents who rarely monitor their children's activities and provide little support may be encouraging delinquent behavior. Be involved in your children's education. Know their teachers. Let the teachers know you expect your children to do well in their class work and you want to be informed immediately of any problems.

4. Discipline effectively. That means discipline in love. Be sure there is a constructive message involved and that the child understands clearly what the proper behavior is. Discipline that doesn't teach how to avoid the behavior in the future not only is useless, it is cruel.

The younger the child engaging in violent or delinquent behavior, the more likely the child will get into more serious trouble later. Which is why it is important to right the child immediately. Everyone makes mistakes but when we and our children acknowledge our errant ways, take responsibility for our actions and learn from them, we can celebrate.

5. Set a good example. Don't send mixed messages about beating Uncle Sam out of a few dollars at tax time, then expect your children not to cheat. Don't have a friend "fix" a traffic ticket and then expect them to respect the justice system.

6. Take the situation seriously. Although there is a big difference between spray painting "Principal Friendly is a dweeb" on the schoolyard wall and cracking an old person's head with a ball bat, some experts say it's probably best to fix equal weight onto each delinquent act. That way parents won't send a message that some things are bad, and others are less bad.

When your child takes an emotional hit

Nothing causes a parent more pain than seeing his or her child suffering. We want to take the hurt ourselves and "make it better." When our child is being smacked emotionally by friends, teachers, or coaches we want to absorb the hits. We want to intervene whenever we possibly can.

And yet, sometimes intervening can make things worse for your child. How do you know when to step in and protect, or stand back, biting your lip and letting your child work things out for himself so that he can grow in the process?

First, don't be overprotective. Children who are always rescued soon learn to assume that they have to be rescued, that they don't have the courage to stand on their own or think they have the ability to care for themselves. Then, when their rescuers are absent or fail, they don't know any emotional position except that of victim—a helpless victim.

Young people who can navigate the social system were empowered early in life with a sense that they had some control over what happened to them. You see this in many of the children at Baptist Children's Homes. They may have other problems but most of them are not afraid to take on any challenge life throws them. They are anything but passive.

Products of healthy homes also have a confidence that allows them to stand against the crowd when the crowd is being stupid, to find reasons for hope when they face a devastating situation.

It's easy to know when and how to intervene to help helpless infants. But children as young as two or three crave within themselves a personal space. Automatic, immediate interventions can hinder their development. If we help them too much, we're overprotective and smothering; too little and we're insensitive and uncaring.

To begin to know when to intervene, and to what degree, the best thing is to gather as much information as possible. Say, "Tell me what happened." This may be easier to do with a preschooler than with a nine or 12-year-old, who is more likely to give a hint of a problem and then clam up.

Be wary of forcing a child to discuss something he obviously doesn't want to talk about. What you mean as concern can be felt as prying. Be sensitive to timing, your tone of voice, and your body language. Simply stating, "Let's talk later, let me know when you're in the mood for me to listen" leaves the channels open. If that fails, try engaging her in an activity to foster camaraderie and thus encourage a conversation.

Acting without enough information has many dangers, starting with embarrassing yourself or your child. It could be that you have misread the situation and issues; there may not be a problem where you see one, or you may be missing the real problem.

Obviously we are more likely to overreact when we don't have a full story. In the elementary years, our panic can make a child unduly frightened since young children pick up and amplify the emotions of their parents.

With a teenager, your overreaction has the opposite effect: "You're doing all the worrying for me; why do I need to bother?"

Parents who typically underreact don't take their children's issues seriously enough, a danger even more common in families where both parents work. Lack of time can prompt you to deny a problem or wish it away. Since we don't have the time or emotional resources to solve the problem, it is tempting to go into denial.

A child whose problems consistently are ignored can feel unsupported, which can jeopardize your relationship and put the child at risk.

The other extreme: parents typically intervene too much and too often in sibling issues. This area is a prime candidate to benefit from the "No Harm, No Foul" brand of justice. Unless they are hurting each other, give them time to work things out on their own.

Here are some guidelines for when to intervene:

- When your child's health, safety, or well-being is at risk
- When he's excessively frustrated and about to give up
- When she asks for legitimate help
- When he withdraws: "I never want to play with Tim again."
- When you see pre-delinquent or illegal behavior
- When he's already tried on his own with no success

However, just because you identify that help is needed doesn't necessarily mean you should take over and solve the problem. You can take it seriously without taking action by being empathetic and repeating back what you hear the youth saying.

Before you go further, experts suggest asking these questions:

- How close is he to resolving the problem on his own?
- Does she have the tools to do it (verbal skills, for instance)?
- Does she know where to start?

Instead of intervening for your child, your best help is often to give your child the coping skills he or she needs to take care of the problem himself. Role play the situation to help your child come up with a witty, deflective comment, or learn the words he needs to apologize or open the conversation with his teacher or the friend who has pushed him outside the circle.

Now you're becoming a coach, saying helpful things like, "Maybe there's another way to look at this? What do you think you could do next time?" and cheerleader, "I have lots of confidence in you!"

The brainstorming step is important, even if the end result is that you are going to intervene, after all. The child needs to feel involved, that she's contributed to the decision.

Checklists for parents

- When you might intervene for one child may not be the same point at which you intervene for another.
- In the school-age years, children are often better able to handle interventions from the same-sex parent.
- Steps to help your child take:
  - ◆ articulate the problem

◆ think of solutions and possible outcomes
● Choose one to attempt

(You can do this even with preschoolers, as long as you do it in a way that's age-appropriate: "I see the two of you can't agree. What do you think is happening here? Oh, so you both want the same toy? What do you think you should do?" Always prepare the child for the possibility that the solution may not work. "If it doesn't, we'll think of something else." But sometimes, nothing works. That's frustrating for any child, but especially for elementary-age kids who expect parents to solve all problems. When you do reach a dead end, be sure to process that: "I'm frustrated, too, but at least we tried everything we could.")

● Intervention that tries to wrest total control from a child almost always backfires, especially with teenagers. When a situation feels beyond your control (drugs, sex, alcohol, theft, violence), seek professional help.

Teens growing up scared

Adults face fear with an arsenal of defenses at their disposal. They can measure the threat against their ability to withstand it. They are bigger, stronger, and faster. They're insured, experienced, and they have a support network.

America's young people, on the other hand, surrounded by such problems as violence and drugs, are growing up scared, according to researcher George Gallup's book, *Growing Up Scared in America and What the Experts Say Parents Can Do About It.*

Gallup organized his findings around four "at-risk" behaviors which make for a frightening world: violence, sex, health issues, and drug and alcohol addiction. At the end of each chapter, he includes advice gleaned from interviews with leading authorities about how to deal with each of the risk behaviors. Life as a young person should be fun, free, and safe. For too many, across every definable spectrum, it is not.

One of the very best words a young person can use to describe his or her home, or surrogate home, is "safe."

I often think of some the young people I've come to know and love. Lonnie saw his father shoot and kill his mother. Cliff endured almost nightly beatings until he was 15. Malinda's mother's boyfriend pushed dishes of food onto the porch for her and called her a dog. Roberta was beaten with 2x4s.

Is it any wonder teenagers are "scared?"

Some of the fear that grips teenagers' shoulders like the talons of a hunting falcon result from their own risky behaviors. Others haunt them because of the neighborhoods they live in, dangers in undisciplined schools and homes, and families that are not functioning in a healthy manner.

I know there are many youths who are and will continue to be called "problem children." However, I still prefer to say, "They are children with problems." The difference is profound. Those problems are often caused by real situations that strike fear into their hearts, and would scare anyone facing similar demons.

Many "children with problems" have adopted behaviors that are valid to deal with those fears, but are not appropriate behaviors in "polite society." It's best to deal with the fears, help them identify the problems, and lead them to grow in the value Gallup said is most needed to fight the risks: character. To wit:

● Twenty-eight percent of teens say they know peers who have carried or regularly carry guns and knives in school.

● One teen in four says, within the past 12 months, there was at least one time when he or she feared for his or her physical safety while in school classrooms or hallways, on playgrounds, or walking to and from school. The tragic school shootings and deaths in 1998 and 1999 give stark reality to these fears.

● On the home front, 26 percent of teens say they have been hit or physically harmed by a parent or by another adult in the household in the past year. (And this does not include verbal or psychological violence.)

● Unwanted pregnancies and AIDS make teen sexuality more complicated—and more dangerous—than ever. Fifty-three percent of high school students have engaged in sexual intercourse. One in 11 abortions performed in the United States is performed on a woman age 18 or under.

● Bad eating habits, not enough sleep and exercise, and too much fatty food combine to put America's teens on a dangerous path.

● Rampant drug and alcohol abuse among teens is linked not only to higher rates of juvenile crime but also to rising rates of teen suicide. The five biggest factors leading to suicide are drug abuse, not getting along with parents, peer stresses, problems of growing up, and alcohol abuse.

● Fifty-nine percent of teens know someone who has attempted suicide; 26 percent know someone who has succeeded; 55 percent have discussed the topic with friends; 37 percent have considered taking their own lives.

● Nearly half (46 percent) of American teens say that drinking is a problem among their peers.

Kids' cries drown in cultural noise

In a noisy world, whimpering cries for help are often lost in the blaze of sound that consumes all the timbre of silence around us. The blare of television, the jangling telephone, snarling traffic, pounding stereos in cars next to us, discmans, walkmans, talkmans, and crazy mans surround us.

Supportive agencies and individuals listen for cries. But too often, the din around us drowns those cries. Who is listening when a young person moans? Who hears a stifled sob or who catches the real pain behind the surface defiance?

Ministers of children and youth in our churches have a huge job. While they are not expected to take the place of all that parents must do, they often represent a non-threatening figure to whom a teen can pour out his or her complaints. Every day, youth ministers hear statements such as these:

"My mom and dad are a pain."
"Why am I fat?"
"Why do I have pimples?"
"Why doesn't anybody like me?"
"Why am I not more athletic?"
"My dad hits me and my mom hates me."
"My coach is a fool."
"Brother treats the dog better than he treats me."
"My boyfriend is pressuring me."
"Everybody smokes."

"I've tried drugs and now I think I'm hooked."

The litany of cries goes on and on as teenagers struggle to become the adults God created them to be. Those who have a helping hand reaching to them while they struggle will make it. Those who cry into a black, empty vacuum will struggle much longer—and their odds of "making it" are significantly lower.

Unfortunately, our society is becoming like the child facing failure and we have a choice to make. We can whimper and convince ourselves we are helpless victims. Or we can soar above the sea of change and help New Millennium Families fulfill their rightful destiny and potential.

Chapter Eleven

Alone in the 'hood: The incredibly hard task of self-cloning

One is the
loneliest number.
   —Three Dog Night

> *I am a hatchling turtle.*
> *I live by the sea.*
> *I was buried,*
> *But still I came to be.*
> *I made my way to the ocean,*
> *And that will be my new home.*
> *Now that my mother has left me,*
> *I am all alone.*
> > *—Wesley, BCH child*

My life is great. My life is good.
But sometimes life is sad,
   Like when my mom is sad.
   But the Lord blessed me
      With a loveable mom.
      My life is full of happiness.
         Even when she is in pain,
            she never takes it out on me.
            My life is wonderful!
               —April, BCH child

This is the shortest chapter in this book. And possibly the most vital.

Though the syntax of these pages uses "parents," each sentence has been constructed under the painful reality that growing numbers of women, and men, in the United States face the daunting challenges of raising children in today's society by themselves.

Those who haven't tried it dare not knock it—or criticize those who do. On a soberly serious level, single mothers and fathers raising families brings to mind the old line about America's greatest dancing couple. "Ginger Rogers did everything Fred Astaire did," the wag goes, "except she did it backwards and in high heels."

Single parents need and are worthy of all possible support. Following are some specific suggestions, keeping in mind that other chapters also contain things they need to do for and with their children.

Children need all the authentic love they can get. Even two parents, working together in the same home, cannot soak a child's sponge-like heart with all the love he can absorb. Imagine then, the difficulty of a single parent providing all the love, attention, daily necessities, and all the answers his or her children need.

With all the needs, but half the personnel, of a mother-father parent set, single parents struggle to deal with their children's need for the missing resources—the love and attention they deserve. Children with an absentee parent need an extra dose of love. If you spend even a few hours with children "in care," you'll hear a love expressed for parents that would touch your inner core.

Somewhat surprisingly, deep love, affection, and longing often are directed toward a parent they barely know: the father who walked out 10 years ago and hasn't been heard from since, except for a very occasional postcard or Christmas phone call; the mother who gave him up for adoption. A common goal "as soon as I get out of here" is to reestablish contact with that missing piece of their heart and childhood.

Among the most joyous moments of my time at BCH have been seeing such things happen.

Cliff had not had contact with his mother for almost 15 years when he came to us. His father, severely emotionally disturbed by his Vietnam experiences, raised his sons to "survive." This included beating them, booby-trapping the house, and giving them a one hour head start in the woods before he began tracking them—with a loaded weapon.

Not only were we allowed to help Cliff overcome much of the emotional damage he had sustained, we also facilitated finding his mother and reuniting them. Today, he lives near her on the West Coast, trying to fill some of those gaping holes left over from a motherless childhood.

Custody parents, often dealing with their own hurts and anger, have a captive audience if they want to rage against their former spouse. But it damages the children. There is a need for honesty and reality, but not for meanness.

Absentee parenthood can take many forms, from abandonment with no contact to semi-regular visits with no emotional connection. How sad to see a father spend most of his weekend visitation on his cell phone or a mother spending more attention on her boyfriend than her visiting son and daughter.

Children with missing parents have the hardest time. To know a parent slightly, but not well enough to see his faults for yourself, leaves the biggest developmental hole in a child's life, potentially even harder to heal from than a parent's death.

It's a sense of knowing, "My father is alive, he's out there, but he chooses not to be with me. What's wrong with me?" It's a thought that can stay with a child for many years. The most common professional advice single parents receive is not far from what they know instinctively: Honesty, in age-appropriate doses, is the best policy.

Typically, children with absentee fathers were abandoned before birth or shortly thereafter. When a father leaves, alcohol or drug abuse is often the reason why. If the mother leaves, it's often because of mental illness—though the number of AWOL mothers because of drug or alcohol is spiraling upward.

No matter what the cause, beginning when your single-parent family is created, even if your child is an infant, tell the story of how your family formed. Don't be brutally frank but don't stray far from the truth. Let the child draw his or her own conclusion about right or wrong. Dealing with being abandoned is tough enough without being rushed into it or being told who to blame.

The more infrequent, unpredictable, and unsatisfying the contact with an absentee parent, the more likely a child is to have fantasies about her/him far removed from reality. The tendency is to build the missing parent up bigger than life, imagining how different things would be "if my dad (or mom) were here."

Don't get defensive or competitive over this. Instead, validate and voice the child's hopes: "I know you wish things were different. I know you miss having a dad. I wish it were different too, but it isn't." Don't instill false hope in your child, even though you want so much for your child to hurt less. It's better to deal honestly with the disappointments the absentee parent dishes out.

Starting when your child is a toddler, talk about how families are different. "Sometimes, both parents live together, sometimes the children live with the dad and see the mom only sometimes. In our family . . . ."

A child with an absentee parent tends to need frequent reinforcement that you love her just the way she is. Tell her often that nobody wants her to be a different person. As she gets older, be more explicit: "It's not that if you were more athletic or smarter, or a boy instead of a girl, your dad would be around more. This isn't about you, it's about what he is able to do."

Such children can be clingy so try to tolerate the difficulty around separations and reinforce your stability. With a preschooler: "I'll be here when you wake up and every other morning, too." With an older child: "Your father and I are separate people. I am not going to make the choice he did. I want to stay with you. Being your parent is my most important job." You cannot say too often to your child, single parent or not, "I love you." They never get enough. *No matter how old they are!!*

What Single Parents Can Do

- Make photos of the absentee parent available. Some children like to have a place where they can keep photos or mementos.
- Don't bad-mouth the parent. Sooner or later, a child begins to understand that he/she is half that person and worries: "If he's a liar and a cheat, maybe I am, too."
- Not talking about the person at all is equally bad, giving rise to inappropriate fantasies.
- For your child's sake, rise above your own feelings and find some neutral things to say about the absentee parent.
- Contact with members of the parent's extended family is OK, even beneficial, as long as they won't undermine you or glorify him.

• It doesn't matter what your child calls an absentee parent but don't be surprised if an older child stops referring to him as "dad" and starts calling him by name. As he grasps the degree of emotional distance, that may seem more authentic to him.

• Commemorate a parent's birthday to acknowledge his existence and open a conversation. Light a candle and say simply, "We don't know where you are, but we hope you're well."

• With a young child who wants to talk to his parent, encourage a pretend conversation: "What would you say if you could talk to her? What do you want her to say back to you?"

• Don't belittle fantasies a child shares or she may never do it again. Try instead to gently insert some reality. "You wish he really was a person who brought you presents, don't you?"

• Teenagers of absentee parents typically worry about their relationships: "Am I holding onto this boyfriend because I love him or because I can't stand another abandonment?"

Single parents, you have a tough row to hoe. Don't be hesitant to seek counseling or other adults to mentor your child. Talk to your minister in confidence about ways the church could be more supportive of single parents. Take care of your spiritual needs and seek out Christian friends who can support you and whom you can support.

Chapter Twelve

Two tragic evils:
child abuse,
drug abuse

Sad things can happen in your life,
And you can never give them away.
—*Keisha, BCH child*

Everyone needs to work together
and get along.
It's us kids who have to deal with it.
and that's wrong.
But if everyone can't get along
and work together
We will be that way
forever.
—*Chrissy, BCH child*

My head has shrunk
Shrunken so small
Even the keenest eye could not see anything
But the loneliness in the paths of my soul.
My body has left
Left all the veins alone in the darkness once again
The night has fallen upon my shoulders
Mistaken me for the follower
But this time I will not follow the falling of the night.
—*Amy, BCH child*

These are not good days for America's children.

One of eight children in America under age 12 is hungry—that's five and a half million kids. I'm not talking about between-meal snack hunger. I'm talking about an ache tonight that won't go away tomorrow. And hunger is only one malaise assailing our children.

One of four children under age six lives in poverty and suffers the attendant mental, emotional, and physical insults. Every eight seconds of the school day, a child drops out. Every 26 seconds, a child runs away from home. Every 47 seconds, a child is abused or neglected. Every 67 seconds, a teenager has a baby. Every seven minutes, a child is arrested for a drug offense. Every 36 minutes, a child is killed or injured by a gun. Every day 135,000 children bring their own guns to American schools.

Every day, every minute, defenseless, innocent, trusting children are assaulted. They are burned with cigarettes for crying too loudly; they are scalded with hot cooking oil for messing their diapers; they are forced to drink water until their brains hemorrhage because they were unruly.

A headline in a major American newspaper read, "Children get poorer, nation gets richer." The subhead said, "Americans have to have the discipline to make those investments in our youth." Sometimes our restrictive laws make it too difficult to remove a child at risk of abuse or neglect from its "at risk" environment. There is just too little willingness on our part to change things. This must stop. We must wake up and save this generation of children now.

Tomorrow is too late. The horror must be halted!

Consider some American facts:

● Deaths from child abuse continue to increase. Routinely some deaths are so horrible that few newspapers print the gruesome details.

● Annually there are one million confirmed cases of abuse and neglect.

● Annually 1,300 abused kids die—even though 42 percent had been reported earlier to child protective agencies.

● Each day in our country—and all these statistics are conservative—10 children die from gunshots and 30 are wounded.

● Each day six children commit suicide and 3,000 run away from home.

● Nearly 23 percent of our kids, 15.7 million, live in poverty. This persistent grinding deprivation leaves them hungry, shabby, or sick; ill prepared for school; and lonely in one-parent homes that often are frequently buffeted by crime.

America certainly has the resources to fight this war, but do we have the will? A national report on my desk reads: "We're on the verge of admitting it's a losing battle. Until the United States of America adopts a philosophy that our children are as important as bridges, roads, and prisons, we're never going to have the resources necessary to meet the needs."

Just like you, I don't want the government poking its nose into every part of my daily life. But if a government is for anything, it is to provide for the common defense and well-being of its people. We cannot be a "well people" without an educated, safe generation of children.

Many adults are insulated from the needs of children. Children have no political power. They do not vote; they do not organize into pressure groups; they do not plan protest marches on governments. Their opinions carry little weight. They are virtually dependent upon adults to act in their best interests and protect their rights.

Children need advocates. Orphanages, homes for children, and other foster care agencies have been historic advocates for children. But we're not enough. Government must assume a partnership role with agencies caring for dependent children. Child care agencies face the double whammy of increasing costs for care and decreasing streams of revenue to provide it. Government agencies ask us to do more and more with children, while paying only about half the cost of their care.

Adults must become their advocates, their protectors, their friends. Don't let your elected representatives make unwise decisions that will lose this generation. How will you operate your business in 10 years from now when the average new job will require 13.5 years of education—but we have a 28 percent high school dropout rate?

America has the money, but somehow, roads and criminals and international conflicts have muscled ahead of our weak and innocent children. "The real crisis," says Warren Nord of the University of North Carolina at Chapel Hill, "is that too many of our children use outhouses, are raised in poverty, are attempting suicide, are using drugs, are killing each other off. They aren't learning what's important, while we sit on our bank accounts, while we imbue our children with mindless consumerism and make a fetish of wealth. We have lost sight of the mountains for all the pollution in the valley."

Some of you are business professionals. You represent economic muscle. You must realize that your business will suffer with an undereducated work force. You must be a part of the solution. For example:

- The Business Roundtable, with representatives from the largest 200 companies, made support for education its highest priority in the 1990s. It is hoped this will continue in the new millennium.
- In Dallas, Texas Instruments helps fund the local Head Start Program.
- In Des Moines, IA, business leaders sponsor a program called *Smoother Sailing*, which sends counselors into the city's elementary schools.

I wrote earlier that my desire to speak out was a cumulative call. Let me tell you one of the whispers I heard.

A girl came into our care who was the victim of ignorance. She was a darling child, but her eyes did not glow with the wonder of new learning or awe of fresh experience. Instead, they burned with fear and suspicion.

This child's family used her for sport. They would put the four-or five-year-old in the middle of the room and sit in a circle around her, each with a cigarette lighter or a match. They touched fire to her arms or legs and laughed as she reeled crying from one edge of the circle to another.

One day they were too careless and the girl's clothes caught fire, endangering her life and badly scarring her body. Hospital personnel alerted social workers, who placed her in our care. Later, I was sitting with this little girl's child care worker who told me the child had said, "No one could love me. I'm too ugly."

I put my arms around her and, behind tear-filled eyes, told her, "God loves you, darling. And I love you, too."

I'm not asking the government to love our children. I'm not asking you to love all children. But I do pose this question: what is our condition when thousands of children are abused and run away? Thousands more have psychological problems that often result in suicide. Another vast number look around and say, "No one loves me."

That's where we are today in America and, unfortunately, in much of the world. If we leave it for someone else to do, or say we'll fix things tomorrow, that's where we'll be next year, too.

Some children abused before birth

I hate to admit it, but I cannot help every child who needs help. I wish I could. Because of licensing requirements, my organization is limited to accepting only children of school age into residential care.

This leaves out a large number of preschool children who are neglected by a mother or parents, too consumed with bad habits or survival to care for the child. It is not uncommon for us to learn of four-year-olds struggling to care for younger siblings.

Horribly, there exists an even younger group of abused children: infants who are abused "from their first breath." These children became addicted to horrible drugs while still in the womb, babies poisoned by their own mothers.

Statistics predict the mother will give the same welcoming gift to her next child and may already have subjected any earlier babies to the same horror.

That is the way it is: poison one child, poison another, keep them all. It's one of the liberties permitted by American culture and law.

Some babies recover in a few months or a year. But with many, the price of abuse can last through years of slow learning, erratic behavior, behavior-control drugs administered by frustrated parent or school, unmanageable behavior, low expectations, and an often tumultuous ride through the foster care system.

These children will exhibit some symptoms of hard-core drug addicts. But the way our system handles these desperate problems puzzles many observers, and it puzzles me.

If police, hospitals, or caseworkers found a mother injecting drugs into the bloodstream of a six-year-old, they would remove the child from that abusive mother and probably send the mother to jail.

Yet consider what happens when blood tests taken after birth prove not only that the baby was poisoned by drugs while still in the womb, but also prove that Mommy was so hard core she took heroin or cocaine just before labor. What happens? We return the baby to its abuser and just pick up the bills for special treatment or classes as long as the baby needs them.

The sad reality is that the newborn baby infused with drugs as a fetus is as abused as an older child given heroin or crack. We need to ask a hard question: has the philosophy of child welfare been too rigidly focused on only holding families together even at the cost of protecting children?

Families are sacred and central. Salvaging and repairing the family is always our primary goal at Baptist Children's Homes. But "family" needs to be defined in spiritual terms. Genetic connections and DNA relationships are all but meaningless if the parent is so disturbed—or so evil—-that there is no emotional investment in the happiness and welfare of the child.

That needs to change.

A newborn child who has drugs in his system and is, in fact, addicted, should be considered a victim of abuse. A mother who forces her unborn child to draw nourishment from a blood stream polluted with drugs proves she is incapable of making the proper decisions about her baby's safety. She can be expected to mistreat it as it grows older, and abuse her other children as well. As far as the child is concerned, it doesn't matter if the mother uses drugs because she is addicted, or is in a situation where she is pressured to do so, or is simply ignorant of the danger of her actions. Our cultural priorities should be:

1. protect the baby;

2. help the woman get control of her life,

3. see if the mother and child can be reunited later, but only in a safe and healthy relationship.

Paying attention to the abused newborn would bring more attention to the rest of the family and its safety.

Meanwhile, some people want to legalize mood enhancing/altering drugs. They call drug use a "victimless crime." Most of the robberies and killings associated with drugs occur because drugs are hard to get, and therefore expensive. The demand allows incredible "mark-up" so that dealing is a highly profitable—and obviously untaxed—business.

If they were legal and easily available at the local "drug store," the price would drop and crime associated with drugs would almost disappear, they say. But, given the babies born addicted, would such drug legalizers demand that every woman pass a non-pregnant test to get drugs, or pass a drug test every week until childbirth?

If she failed, what then? Forced abortion? Or just let mothers who will not control their addiction pass its evil on to their babies before they draw breath?

No child is an island

As tragic and horrible as the prenatal drug abuse of children and the battering of children by drug-addicted adults are, the evil well of child abuse would not dry up even if substance abuse were completely eliminated.

With information flooding our senses every day from around the world, it seems to take tragedies of enormous magnitude to affect us. We hardly raise our heads from our morning coffee to read that hundreds died in a South American hurricane, or thousands of Albanians are murdered in ethnic cleansing, or a monsoon-induced mudslide erases a village in Asia, or drought decimates the African sahel.

Instead we have our ear tuned to the traffic report so we know which snarled intersection or slow-moving freeway to avoid on our way to work.

We can read about, listen to, and observe serious flaws in the fabric of "family" in our nation and think, "Thank God, our kids are OK", and go right on without missing a beat. It takes enormous statistical tragedies to shake us awake. Or else very personal, firsthand knowledge.

Unmoved to learn that hundreds of children in America died last year from abuse and neglect, we sigh and shake our heads at the report of a baby in our town whose parents shook him to death because he wouldn't stop crying. Oblivious to children in our own community becoming death-by-abuse victims, we can become outraged upon learning that a five-year-old was found caring for his three siblings in a filthy, rat-infested shack in another part of the country.

Blinded to the more than three million children who were reported as possible mistreatment victims last year, we are angered to indigestion to learn of an infant being dumped in a trash bin behind the local hotel.

Because of sensory overload, compassion fatigue, and emotional filters, confronting the brutally cold statistics of children beaten and killed every day may not automatically grab your attention and your heart. But I hope you will make the mental effort to confront them and then move to participate in the fight against abuse. You will be moved to invest in children's lives by investing with those who are seeking to make a difference.

It may not move you to know that child mistreatment is connected to drug and alcohol abuse, parents who don't understand the stages of child development, have no parenting skills, suffer from financial stress, and indulge in domestic violence.

It would, if you knew Jolene. Because her biological mother could not control her own drug and alcohol addictions, she released Jolene for adoption. When her adoptive parents exhibited the same lack of self-control, Jolene was left virtually on her own on the brink of her teen years. She wonders what authentic adults she can find who will care for her and help her to become the woman God created her to be. Maybe BCH can provide that or, maybe, God has positioned you to do that.

Signs of potential child abuse

By law, if you suspect child abuse, you must report it to the proper authorities. But statutes are poor reasons for moral actions. Jesus talked about those who harm "little ones" and he spoke harshly. The Bible also indicts those to "know to do good and do it not." If we neglect to protect a child from abuse when we have knowledge and opportunity, we stand condemned.

Here are some warning signs that may point to abuse or neglect:
- Bruises, burns, or other unexplained injuries
- Sick children who haven't received medical care
- Children who are hungry and frequently don't seem to get enough food
- Children frequently left unsupervised
- Children with access to things such as drugs or alcohol

Seek the counsel of your pastor or godly friends, take advantage of "your identity will be protected" programs, if necessary. It is not easy to accuse someone of child abuse—but it is a serious matter to let children suffer. Remember that you don't have to have definite knowledge of child abuse, just certainty that warning signs are present. The life you save may mean your morning coffee tomorrow won't be interrupted by another too-close-to-home report of the death of another too young, too innocent, too defenseless victim.

Battling an epidemic of child violence

It's the stuff of horror movies. Two high school boys, often seen in black trench coats, move through their school and murder 13 people before killing themselves. But this story isn't fiction. The 1999 tragedy at Columbine High School in Littleton, Colo., burned into the national collective memory like the assassination of John F. Kennedy in 1963 and the explosion of the Challenger spacecraft in 1986.

Baby Boomers recite the time, date, and place they learned of the shooting in Dallas; Generation X'ers recall the same details as their minds replay the stunning spiral of smoke shortly after Challenger's launch—"Go with the throttle up." The Millennials will peg their shared history around a boy dangling from a second story window after being shot in the head, as SWAT team members reach to rescue him.

The murderous rampage brought international attention to the increasingly worrisome problem of violent children.

What pushes a youngster to commit acts we once thought only adult psychopaths would consider? I'm not alone when I shake my head and admit that adults will be afraid of children in the new millennium. But working where I do, I learn many of the contributing causes to young people turning violent.

The intake studies of the boys and girls at BCH tell of young lives scarred by violence observed as well as violence absorbed. This boy repeatedly watched his father beat his mother unconscious. This one hid under the couch as his mother cut her sleeping boyfriend's throat. That girl was standing on a street corner when a drive-by shooter gunned down two of her friends. That one saw her sister raped.

Some young people think that it's a form of entertainment or "fun," to hit each other over the head with a baseball bat or gouge somebody's eyeball. Video clips of teenagers performing professional wrestling stunts in their back yards—but for real—stun the viewer. They leap off buildings onto each other and barbed wire and broken glass. They smash metal chairs over each other's backs and crack 2x4's over each other's heads.

Contrast that to the childhood activities of my now grown son and daughter. Happy sounds—of trucks roaring down the carpet freeway, building blocks tumbling from the sofa skyscraper, cowboys galloping through the hallway forest, and plastic dishes clattering from the teahouse bedroom—filled the house. When they got rough with each other or with friends, the villains, super-heroes, and other formidable creatures they fashioned were merciful in their "killings," and victims laughed and rose to fight again.

Times change. Today I think most kids could recite to you what is right and wrong, but whether they have the self-control to stop themselves from doing something wrong is another question.

Many counselors work with families in which violence has been a factor. Most often it is with the child as victim, not as perpetrator. But, increasingly, children are the perpetrators. Often before a really severe act is committed, there is a pattern of escalating violence, giving anyone who observes it a chilling feeling that something awful will happen if the pattern is not interrupted.

Children talk to counselors or teachers about wanting to strangle their baby siblings. Kids are in foster care because they've taken life-threatening actions against other children. Child psychologists tell of young clients revealing unspeakable acts with no sign of remorse: urinating in a soda bottle and giving it to a friend, boiling a turtle and watching it slowly die, setting the family's garage on fire.

Sadly, such things seem but a reflection of our society. Sad—and frightening.

Once a child has gone so far as to commit a vicious, violent act, many experts believe the only hope for changing the behavior is removal from the home setting, intense therapy, and often, medication. Even then, the prognosis is far from rosy.

Children who seem "too bad to be true" often are diagnosed with Conduct Disorder, a psychological term that describes youngsters who are physically and verbally aggressive. The disorder usually appears before age six or after age ten. The later it is diagnosed, the worse the prognosis because it is very difficult to treat.

In such cases, you certainly do need help. *Don't be afraid to seek it.* If your child is strangling cats, mercilessly beating smaller neighbors, or constantly threatening physical harm to siblings, treat it seriously. Better to find help today than to arm ourselves for our own protection tomorrow. Even better, take measures to protect children from reaching that psychological state.

The first step is: don't despair. There is a reason we think of the future as "bright" no matter how dark the past. Because the promise of tomorrow is hopeful. And, as we discuss in our closing chapter, tomorrow is also grace-full.

Chapter Thirteen

A grace-full future:
God's promise embraces
New Millennium Families

I am not afraid of storms, for I am learning to sail my ship.
—Louisa May Alcott

My old flannel, all raggy and worn,
Has been through it all—sunshine and storm.
The sun and the rain have beat my old friend down,
And now it's fading and showing its days.
It's kind of like me—I've been through it all and
Am still hanging around.
It gives me encouragement and even some pride,
But it was all up to me since I had to decide.
—Kim, BCH child

Lord, my Father, I'm asking you tonight,
To let my soul shine good and bright.
I love you Lord, with all my heart.
I'll tell you what, I'm going to keep smart.
I better go, Lord, and go to sleep.
Thank you for saving my soul.
I'll try not to weep.
I love you, Lord and Good-night.
P.S. I'll shine bright.
—Angie, BCH child

"It's always darkest before the dawn." That comforting truth helps a lot of us "hang on" during tough times. But future light can't keep us from banging our shins now on unseen rocks or stumbling into briar patches in the blackness.

The pain and hurt—and potential for major damage if we insist on running wildly when we can't see what is in front of us and around us—are real. But the arriving sunrise lets us see our wrong turns, begins to heal our bruises, and lets us connect with others-who've-dwelt-in-darkness in supportive community.

But those gifts come only if our eyes open to the light. Imagine the foolishness of a haggard, battered pilgrim surviving—if only barely—the night, only to squint his eyes against the golden streaks streaming over the horizon. Is that you?

It is a dark, dark night for America's family and children. The statistics are too staggering, the damage too widespread, the faces and cries of the hurting too haunting to pretend otherwise.

But the dawn is before us. We can draw courage because of that truth. That bright morning is wrapped in the wonderful and sustaining mystery of God's loving grace. It's there.

"Be still," Grace whispers, "and know that I am God. Walk carefully in the darkness, remember the safe paths you learned in prior days of sunshine, and search for them. And strain your heart and eyes toward the coming dawn."

Our human nature chants, "this darkness is forever, it doesn't get any better than this, save yourself (if you can)." Grace says, "My light will overcome every darkness."

Pause in the pitch-blackness of your troubled marriage or family. If you listen keenly, you may hear the ragged breathing of a sobbing, fellow struggler. A fellow named David. David, the lion and bear and giant killer. David, the King and poet. David, the murderer. David, the adulterer and horrid husband. David, the failed father. David, the man "with a heart like God."

Talk about your dysfunctional family!

David, the most visible Hebrew success story, also is Israel's greatest private failure in his closest relationships. He burst on the scene in a glow of patriotic glory by standing boldly before Goliath and striking him down with a slingshot. His military genius united the prickly tribes of Israel into a coherent and powerful nation. His popularity made "Saul has slain his thousands and David his ten thousands" number one on the Jerusalem hit parade. As administrator, public opinion manipulator, strategist and visionary, he was the man.

His musical ability could soothe any anguish, his poetry served as the foundation for Jewish high and holy worship. He was Colin Powell,

Donald Trump, Michael Jordan, the Beatles, and Abraham Lincoln rolled into one.

The only superlatives that match his public persona describe his private life—and then the superlatives are all negative.

There is no indication that any of his eight wives or numerous mistresses ever meant anything to him. His marriages mixed a touch of fleeting sexual excitement with a generous helping of political savvy. No compassion or tenderness seemed to surround any of his personal relationships, though he did care deeply for a non-relative, his "best buddy," Jonathan.

David embarrassed his throne and his God with adultery. He let his lust rule him. He stole Bathsheba from her husband, Uriah, and then had that loyal and brave captain abandoned on the battlefield so he would be killed. That was just the most infamous of many actions he incorrectly felt were "private" and had no application to his public being.

David's relationship with his children was an unparalleled disaster, a not uncommon occurrence when a man fails to truly love the mother of his sons and daughters. One of his sons committed incest with his sister, which promptly inspired another brother to kill him. David's spoiled, favorite son, Absalom, led a military revolt against his father, chasing him out of Jerusalem and into the wilderness before David could rally his army.

One of the most morose stories in the Bible recounts David weeping and mourning after learning that, in direct violation of his orders, Absalom has been killed, stabbed as he dangled from a tree by his long, curly hair.

But enough of the story of David—as long as we remember that his life and reputation were redeemed to the point that Jesus was called "The Son of David" and was the spiritual fulfillment of God's promise that David's descendants would rule over a spiritual Israel forever.

Read it and study it in-depth for yourself. But you get the general idea. Public successes do not create private happiness. It is the story of so many today. The CEO or foreman who inspires those he supervises to ever higher levels of production fails to earn the respect of his teenage daughter.

Athletes with salary enough to purchase their own small country vainly seek joy and peace in crack cocaine. Women with the finest bodies, wardrobes, skin, hair, and style money can buy write horrid books about their horrid childhood or, worse, poetry about the meaninglessness of life. The public face is a facade, a fake front. Yet behind the shells are puzzled husbands and wives, sons and daughters, who live in an emotional and spiritual darkness they think is permanent. They have too little—or no—faith that dawn is possible; no understanding that Someone greater than David loves them and their family and their marriage.

Most of us are sophisticated sinners. I use the category "sinner" not to imply that we all live particularly evil or degraded lives, but the way Jesus utilized it. In his rating system, which fully discounts our stock portfolios, hair color, and waist lines, we all are persons standing in need of grace.

Unlike us, Jesus didn't look at men and women and see labels like "conservative" or "liberal," "business" or "labor," "hip" or "nerd." He always saw a human being whose life was incomplete without the grace that lifts people into the Father's family. In other words, he saw them— and sees us—running around in the dark.

He knows and understands that behind the fashionably dressed, outwardly successful, seemingly self-assured person lurks a frightened, confused individual whose personal relationships are in shreds and whose mind is clouded with doubts, unsure of his or her real worth and unhappy with her or his future prospects. Just like the folks our society declares "unsuccessful."

Jesus had a word for a woman who could have been the poster child for America's Families-Waiting-for-the-Dawn. We know her as the Samaritan woman at the well. She was dangling precariously at the end of a string of failed marriages with a live-in boyfriend. There is no mention of children, but her track record doesn't speak of stable mother-child relationships. The woman was isolated; she didn't come to the well in the cool of the evening with other women.

Jesus, by offering "living water" so that she would never thirst, was saying that life finds its true fulfillment only inside the family of God. Only when we let the Perfect Parent love us and nurture us and lead us.

The word for this? *Grace.*

Many seeming successful people have a string of broken and fractured relationships. Successful in the world, they are abject failures as loving human beings. Yet, the brightest rays of that coming dawn is Jesus' open invitation that reaches from a water hole in the Middle East to every home in the world, from the simplest believer to the most sophisticated cynic.

The word for this? *Grace.*

No one can fully separate his or her life into "public" and "private" domains. No one fits neatly into "good" or "bad" categories, for no one is so bad as to be beyond the reach of God's restoration. And no one is so good as to not need it.

The word for this? *Grace.*

We are designed to celebrate the sunrise, to walk and love and live in the light of joy-filled marriages, strong families, and rich friendships. God certified his creation as good, marriage as a wonderful benefit, and children as a blessing.

In the context of this book, an appropriate acronym for Grace is: **G**od's **R**iches **A**t **C**hrist's **E**xpense.

Our families and marriages have access to riches we cannot comprehend because Jesus Christ defeated the darkness and made possible our adoption into the family of God. In that family are people who have painfully mapped out the paths you can follow in the dark— and they'll hold your hand and walk with you. In that family are brothers and sisters who will listen to your hurts and confusion and help you open your eyes to the light you have shut out.

I'm glad that that family is mine and that I am that family's. I rejoice that Baptist Children's Homes of North Carolina has heavenly orders to be a place of refuge in the darkness for thousands of children, mothers and fathers. And that we get to see so many of our close relatives greet new dawns in their relationships.

I am confident that New Millennium Families are designed and destined to soar above the flood of changes in the coming centuries because:

● People want to change for the better. God created humans to be in God's image.

● Other people can help people change. God said it is not good for us to be alone.

● As an individual, "I" can help others change. Jesus said to love one another.

● God is the source of real, lasting change. He is the way, the truth, and the light.

The word for my confidence in New Millennium Families? Grace!

Epilogue

Before you soar: helping children deal with fear and horror

The floods will come. When it rains long enough, hard enough, rivers overflow.

Trauma will ambush our children. Evil isn't banished, even by the best parenting.

This book grew out of recognition that bad things happen and a hope we could explore ways to help keep our heads above water. But we'll still deal with flood damage, physical and emotional.

As *New Millennium Families* entered the final editing stages, two events hammered their way into the message: hurricane-driven floods in Eastern North Carolina and brutal, senseless murders in Western North Carolina.

One Sunday morning, a month after the twin horrors, I stood in the pulpit of a church in Greenville, NC, and looked into the tired eyes and strained faces of people having trouble thinking of "the heavens" as a source of blessings.

Weeks of battling the physical and emotional by-products of hurricanes had wearied bodies and tested spirits. They needed a day of rest and a word of hope.

Then it started raining. Eyes turned upward as if capable of seeing through the ceiling to judge the width and depth of this latest threat.

My stomach knotted and my breath quickened. I wondered how the residents of eastern North Carolina could take any more. Naturally, my deepest thought turned to the children and staff at BCH's Kennedy Home in Kinston, NC. Already I had listened to stories of irrational fear when clouds blocked the sun and a summons to lethargy because, "it's just going to flood again anyway."

Meanwhile, folks in the western part of North Carolina didn't give a cloudy day a second thought. But around Waynesville, it suddenly was very important to keep doors locked, even in the daytime. The creaks, thumps and snaps common to rural life lost their charm in

September when five people—three generations of one family—were murdered near BCH's Broyhill Home campus. A classmate, friends and neighbors had been brutally killed for no apparent reason other than chance encounters with evil men.

If I, living in mid-state and geographically distanced from both the watery nightmares of the east and illogical terror of the west, still feel the grinding depression of relentless natural disasters and smell some of the fear in the mountain breezes—what pressures are the people living in the emotional epicenter feeling?

As our staff help their charges deal with these emotions, we all need to be sensitive to signals from our own children, grandchildren or neighborhood children.

After a disaster or tragedy children typically are afraid of four things: that the event will be repeated; someone will be injured or killed; they will be separated from family; they will be left alone.

Any disruption of the regular routine can be deeply threatening to a child. They depend on a daily routine to reassure them that all is right with their world, that the monster will stay put under the bed. They wake up, eat a bowl of cereal, go to school and play with their friends—and expect to do the same the next day. When disaster knocks the schedule off its tracks, they may become very anxious.

At such times a child naturally looks to what used to be called "authority figures." They want to know someone they perceive as powerful is in charge of the threatening situation. How adults react are their keys on how to feel. If we react with alarm, they likely become even more frightened. If we seem defeated, they may panic. If you ever saw your father cry or observed your mother in the grip of overpowering grief, you probably remember similar emotions.

Additionally, children add to the very real dangers vivid products of their own imagination. Don't lightly dismiss these feeling or try to shame them away. You can't banish imaginary demons by logic or commands. The fear they produce is real, even if they are not.

Staying calm and direct, give the child all information he or she can process. Don't vent your feelings on a child. Find another adult to talk with—out of hearing of the child. We need to acknowledge our own fears, but we also have a responsibility to try to control the situation.

Once immediate danger passes, take time to talk with your child. Don't toss an "it will be all right" over your shoulder as you head out the door. They may want to sit in your lap (for the first time in a long time) to get a physical sensation of your protection as well as your voice.

Acknowledge the legitimate fear, ask them what they fear and why. Give them some procedures that will help make them safe, such as not walking through water or how to dial 911. Knowing they have some control will calm them a great deal. It also gives them a concept that their "normal" world is coming back.

Keep them with you if at all possible. It might seem like a good idea to ship them off to Grandma while you shovel mud. But they need as much routine as possible to feel secure. Even the sibling they seem to badger constantly is an anchor of stability when the rest of his or her surroundings are in upheaval. Plus, if you remain in what they feel is a dangerous situation, they easily can imagine you being injured or killed.

Keep your family life as normal as possible. Continue to be firm and fair in maintaining discipline. Again, rules that may irritate them at other times are welcome indicators of stability during crises.

Be alert for signs of mounting distress. Don't delay seeking help from a trusted counselor. "Childish fears" are a lot like "puppy love." They are totally valid emotionally to the child (and the puppy).

Just like those good folks in Greenville, their intellect knows it can't rain forever, that the sun really will shine again. Likewise, the skittish residents around Waynesville will sleep soundly after a while as time does its healing. But knowing and feeling often travel separate roads.

Let's walk beside our children, and our family and friends, where they are, not where we think they should be. When rain or evil comes we can soar above and beyond.

ABOUT THE AUTHOR

Dr. Michael C. Blackwell has been president of The Baptist Children's Homes of North Carolina since July 1, 1983.

His agency is one of the largest of its kind in the nation, serving nearly 2,000 children and 4,000 family members annually. BCH, a multi-service agency, provides programs and services from more than a dozen locations across North Carolina.

He writes and speaks frequently about stress management, personal wellness, leadership, motivation, and, of course, *New Millennium Families*. He is a member of the National Speakers Association and the North Carolina Writers' Network.

Reared in Gastonia, N.C., he received his undergraduate degree from the University of North Carolina at Chapel Hill and three graduate degrees from Southeastern Seminary in Wake Forest, N.C.

Dr. Blackwell lives in Thomasville, N.C., a community "on the right track," located near the geographic center of the Tar Heel State, and known primarily for producing some of the most beautiful furniture in the world.

The author is available for speeches, interviews, advice, or consultation.

Dr. Michael C. Blackwell
PO Box 338
Thomasville, NC 27360
(336) 474-1222

Index